GALEN ON LANGUAGE
AND AMBIGUITY

PHILOSOPHIA ANTIQUA

A SERIES OF MONOGRAPHS
ON ANCIENT PHILOSOPHY

EDITED BY

W. J. VERDENIUS AND J. H. WASZINK

VOLUME XXXI

ROBERT BLAIR EDLOW

GALEN ON LANGUAGE
AND AMBIGUITY

LEIDEN
E. J. BRILL
1977

GALEN ON LANGUAGE AND AMBIGUITY

*An English Translation
of Galen's 'De Captionibus (On Fallacies)'
with Introduction, Text, and Commentary*

BY

ROBERT BLAIR EDLOW

LEIDEN
E. J. BRILL
1977

ISBN 90 04 04869 3

Copyright 1977 by E. J. Brill, Leiden, Netherlands

All rights reserved. No part of this book may be reproduced or
translated in any form, by print, photoprint, microfilm, microfiche
or any other means without written permission from the publisher

PRINTED IN THE NETHERLANDS

To my Mother and Father

CONTENTS

Acknowledgements IX
Preface XI

PART ONE

INTRODUCTION

I. Some Preliminaries: Galen and *De Captionibus* 3
II. The Concept of Ambiguity and its Relation to the Study of Ambiguity 9
III. Aristotle on Fallacy and Ambiguity 17
IV. 'Lexis' and Galen's General Theory of Language . . . 32
V. Galen's Theory of Ambiguity 40
VI. The Sources and Method of Galen's Theory 49
VII. The Stoics on Fallacy and Ambiguity 56
VIII. Synoptic Analysis of *De Captionibus* 69

PART TWO

TEXT AND TRANSLATION

IX. Galen's *De Captionibus*, with English Translation . . . 87

PART THREE

TEXTUAL COMMENTARY

X. Historical and Textual Commentary 117

Bibliography of Ancient and Modern Sources 137
Index 142

ACKNOWLEDGEMENTS

I wish to express my gratitude for the help given me during the various stages of researching and writing this monograph. I am especially indebted to Professor Charles Kahn and Professor Phillip DeLacy of the University of Pennsylvania, who read and criticized the manuscript in an earlier form, and who assisted in the preparation of the translation of *De Captionibus*.

I am grateful to my former colleagues of the Department of Philosophy, University of Maryland at College Park, for their useful comments.

Finally, I would like to thank Mr. Thomas Farinholt who has often come to my assistance with helpful advice and who has, in addition, read through a complete set of proofs.

Washington, D.C.   R.B.E.

PREFACE

This study has grown out of an interest in the philosophy of language in antiquity, and more especially, in the Stoic contribution to Greek theorizing about language. The general plan to reconstruct the Stoic analysis of language as part of the program initiated in the nineteenth century by Schmidt,[1] Zeller,[2] and Steinthal,[3] and more recently reopened by Lukasiewicz,[4] Mates,[5] and Kneale and Kneale,[6] led directly to a detailed study of Galen's *De Captionibus*, a major source of information on the Stoic doctrine of ambiguity in language. This monograph is a record of the fruit borne by research on this Galenic work.

De Captionibus is one of Galen's 118 extant treatises, although Galen is reputed to have written between 500 and 700 volumes.[7] Despite its title, *De Captionibus* (*On Fallacies*) is not a work solely or even primarily on fallacies. Rather it is a treatise on language, and it may be described fairly as one of the last ancient Greek inquiries into the nature of language.

The objectives of this monograph are to reconstruct, to illuminate, and to make accessible to philosophers and scholars alike two neglected chapters in the history of logic and of the theory of meaning—the Galenic and Stoic analyses of ambiguity in language. The introductory essays, the translation, and the textual commentary are each designed with those ends in view. The unveiling of these pioneer efforts to systematize the notion of ambiguity is of interest to contemporary philosophers of language and linguists

---

[1] Rudolph Schmidt, *Stoicorum Grammatica* (Halle: Eduard Anton, 1839).

[2] Eduard Zeller, *The Stoics, Epicureans and Sceptics*, trans. by O. J. Reichel (New York: Russell & Russell, 1962), pp. 70-124.

[3] H. Steinthal, *Geschichte der Sprachwissenschaft bei den Griechen und Römern*, Pt. 1 (Berlin: Ferd Dummlers, 1890), pp. 271-319.

[4] Jan Łukasiewicz, 'Philosophische Bemerkungen zu mehrwertigen Systemen des Aussagenkalkuls,' *Comptes Rendus des Séances de la Société des Sciences et des Lettres de Varsovie* XXIII (1930), 51-77.

[5] Benson Mates, *Stoic Logic* (Berkeley and Los Angeles: University of California Press, 1953), pp. 11-41.

[6] William Kneale and Martha Kneale, *The Development of Logic* (Oxford: Clarendon Press, 1962), pp. 138-58.

[7] The count of 118 extant works is that of John E. Sandys, in *A History of Classical Scholarship*, Vol. I (3rd ed.; Cambridge University Press, 1921), p. 329.

on at least two accounts: first, these ancient theories represent legitimate attempts to explain the same linguistic phenomenon which is today being discussed; and second, Galen's theory provides a general framework within which the analysis of ambiguity may profitably be elaborated.

Needless to say, the intellectual significance of this often ignored Galenic treatise lies principally in the substantive theories it expounds. On the one hand, Galen proposes an original theory of ambiguity—an effort to classify every type of linguistic ambiguity by reference to theoretical principles. To the present day it has yet to be replaced by a general theory that accounts for every linguistic ambiguity.[8] Galen's overlooked achievement is a tribute to his ability as a philosopher of language, and justifies his promotion from 'footnote rank' in histories of philosophy to the rank of philosophers with interesting things to say on certain but not on all topics. Galen has offered in his theory an answer to the question of what sorts of ambiguity can occur in language.

The two other theories contained in *De Captionibus* are of especial interest to the historian concerned with the philosophy of language in antiquity. In Chapter 2 Galen expounds his own general theory of language. Its central doctrine is that the essence of language is to signify and it specifies various degrees of clarity by which language may convey meaning.

In Chapter 4 Galen assumes the role of doxographer and provides the most systematic account of the Stoic theory of ambiguity in our extant tradition. Each of these theories is discussed (and reconstructed) in the Introduction.[9] A separate chapter is devoted to a consideration of the method Galen employs to develop his theory of ambiguity. There the historical inspiration for both the method and its contents is discussed.[10]

Galen's treatise is nominally on fallacies due to language, and their analysis relies on an analysis of the concept of ambiguity. I have provided an essay on the relation between ambiguity and fallacy due to language to resolve certain fundamental issues.[11] An effort is made also to lend more perspective to Galen's analysis

---

[8] Constituent-structure linguists and exponents of transformational grammar in this century analyze grammatical ambiguity, not all ambiguities in language. See *infra* p. 13, n. 14.
[9] See *infra* Chapters IV, V, and VII.
[10] See *infra* Chapter VI.
[11] See *infra* Chapter II.

by expounding Aristotle's teaching on fallacy and ambiguity, which Galen takes as his point of departure in *De Captionibus*.[12]

The synoptic analysis of Galen's treatise is designed to aid the reader in following our philosopher's often obscure line of argument.[13] The English translation given is based entirely on the Gabler edition[14] except where note is made to the contrary, and a reprint of that edition constitutes part of Chapter IX below. The textual commentary that follows is intended (mainly) for the use of the specialist. There historical, philological, and grammatical analyses explain and support the English translation, and scattered related remarks are made which are of relevance to the understanding of the Greek text.

---

[12] See *infra* Chapter III.
[13] See *infra* Chapter VIII.
[14] Carl Gabler, *Galeni Libellus de Captionibus quae per Dictionem Fiunt* (Rostock, 1903).

PART ONE
INTRODUCTION

CHAPTER ONE

SOME PRELIMINARIES:

GALEN AND *DE CAPTIONIBUS*

Galen's *De Captionibus*, or *De Captionibus penes Dictionem* Περὶ τῶν παρὰ τὴν λέξιν σοφισμάτων (*On Fallacies due to Language*) is an introductory text presumably designed for beginners in logic. Stoics would call it a treatise on dialectic, whereas we might be more inclined to say that it covers topics falling under the heading of informal logic, the philosophy of language, or the theory of meaning. The only other extant treatise of Galen's that is strictly on logic, is the *Institutio Logica*,[1] which has recently been explored by J. Mau,[2] J. Kieffer,[3] and Kneale and Kneale.[4] *De Captionibus* on the other hand, has received short shrift in the literature, being alloted but brief mention, description (which is sometimes inaccurate), or quotation, by Kneale and Kneale,[5] Sarton,[6] Sandys,[7]

---

[1] Galen, *Institutio Logica*, ed. by K. Kalbfleisch (Leipzig: Teubner, 1896). Of Galen's monumental treatise, *De Demonstratione*, only fragments are preserved. They are collected by Iwan Müller in 'Über Galens Werk vom wissenschaftlichen Beweis,' in *Abhandlungen der Philosophisch-Philologischen Klasse der Königlich Bayerischen Akademie der Wissenschaften*, Vol. XX (Munich, 1897), pp. 405-78. In the catalogue of his own writings, Galen takes credit for 124 books on grammar, dialectic, and philosophy. (Note that a treatise may be composed of one *book* or two or ten.) Among these numerous writings are commentaries and essays on the works of Plato, Aristotle, Theophrastus, Eudemus, Chrysippus, and other classical and Hellenistic philosophers. See Galen, *De Libris Propriis*, in *Opera Omnia*, ed. by C. G. Kühn, Vol. XIX (Leipzig, 1821-1833), pp. 43-48. (Hereafter it is referred to as the Kühn ed.)

[2] Jürgen Mau, *Galen, Einführung in die Logik: Kritisch-exegetischer Kommentar mit deutscher Übersetzung* (Berlin: Deutsche Akademie der Wissenschaften, 1960).

[3] John S. Kieffer, *Galen's Institutio Logica: English Translation, Introduction, and Commentary* (Baltimore: The Johns Hopkins University Press, 1964).

[4] Kneale and Kneale, (*The Development of Logic*) pp. 182-85.

[5] Kneale and Kneale, p. 182. *De Captionibus* is described in passing as a 'little tract on fallacies.'

[6] George Sarton, *Galen of Pergamon* (Lawrence: University of Kansas Press, 1954), p. 71

[7] J. E. Sandys, (*A History of Classical Scholarship*. Vol. I), p. 329.

Coxe,[8] Schmidt,[9] Prantl,[10] and Hamblin.[11] At least one reason for this is the condition of the Greek text, which as it appears in Kühn's 1827 edition stands in need of further serious editing.[12] The present study, however, is based on a 'new' edition of the text, prepared as a 1903 inaugural dissertation by Carl Gabler, a student of K. Kalbfleisch.[13] In his edition, Gabler has compared the only extant manuscript of *De Captionibus* (the sixteenth century Ambrosian Q3, [M in the apparatus]) with the text as it appears in the Aldine (Venice, 1525[A]), the Froben (Basel, 1558[B]), the Charterian (Paris, 1639-76 [Ch]), and the Kühn (Leipzig, 1821-33 [K]) editions of Galen's works. In addition he provides a full apparatus on each page, a set of textual observations, and an index verborum.

After Hippocrates, Galen is the most distinguished physician in antiquity,[14] but he was also known as a philosopher of considerable reputation and influence, although not of the same stature as Plato, Aristotle, or Chrysippus.[15] Apart from Aristotle, in the Renaissance Galen was the most influential Greek writer on the subject of scientific method.[16] He is now, in addition, recognized as a reputable logician.[17] Born c. 129 A.D. in Pergamon of an

---

[8] J. R. Coxe, *The Writings of Hippocrates and Galen* (Philadelphia: Lindsay and Blakiston, 1846), p. 480. Coxe writes that in *De Captionibus* Galen 'takes notice of the sophisms in conversation . . . .'

[9] R. Schmidt, (*Stoicorum Grammatica*), pp. 52-53.

[10] Carl Prantl, *Geschichte der Logik im Abendland*, Vol. I (Leipzig, Hirzl, 1855), pp. 576-77. Prantl's remarks on *De Captionibus* Chapter 4 seem inaccurate: '. . . an einer anderen Stelle erhalten wir eine Probe der peripatetischen Bestrebungen auch in diesem Zweige der Logik, insoferne Galenus acht Arten der Amphibolie speciell namhaft macht.'

[11] C. L. Hamblin, *Fallacies*, University Paperbacks (London and New York: Methuen & Co., 1970), p. 98.

[12] Galen, *De Captionibus penes Dictionem*, (Kühn ed.) Vol. XIV, pp. 582-98.

[13] A reprint of Gabler's edition may be found *infra* pp. 88-112.

[14] 'Galen,' *Encyclopaedia Brittanica*, 1968, IX, p. 1083.

[15] Galen is mentioned as a philosopher by Alexander of Aphrodisias, in *Commentaria in Aristotelis Topicorum Libros Octo*, ed. by M. Wallies, (Berlin: *Commentaria in Aristotelem Graeca* (henceforth, *C.I.A.G.*)), Vol. II, Pt. 2, p. 549, l. 24.

[16] Neal W. Gilbert, *Renaissance Concepts of Method* (New York: Columbia University Press, 1960), p. xxvi.

[17] I. M. Bocheński, *La Logique de Théophraste* (Fribourg: Collectanea Friburgensia, 1947), p. 20. Bocheński writes, 'Galien était un logicien de marque; très courant de la littérature logique de son temps, assez exact, original même.'

architect-mathematician Nikon, Galen heard lectures of the four principal philosophical schools—the Platonic, Peripatetic, Stoic, and Epicurean.[18] Having studied at Smyrna and Alexandria, he eventually became court physician to Marcus Aurelius Antoninus, and to his heir Commodus. Galen died in 199 A.D.

Galen's father advised him not to be hasty in proclaiming allegiance to any one sect, but rather to inquire for many years without committing himself to a school. By Galen's own admission, he followed this advice.[19] In the nineteenth century literature on Galen, however, he is classified as either an Eclectic Peripatetic [20] (by Zeller) or as a Later Peripatetic [21] (by Prantl). In *De Captionibus* Galen's bias is in favor of Aristotle and Plato and against the Stoics, with no perceptible evidence of Epicurean interest. In *De Placitis* Galen's arguments are by and large against the Stoics and in favor of Plato and Hippocrates.[22] The evidence points to Galen's being in general an Eclectic, but more Platonic than Peripatetic. A more systematic study of Galen's thought is required, however, before any firm conclusion can be drawn in this regard.

De Captionibus is best understood in its philosophical context or setting. It appears to stand squarely in the tradition of studies proposing, identifying, and describing fallacies or invalid arguments. In Greek philosophy, Plato's *Euthydemus* is a pioneer work in the field, whereas Aristotle's *Sophistici Elenchi* is a later, more comprehensive effort. In the *Euthydemus*, we recall, two Sophists, Euthydemus and Dionysodorus, argue by means of their sophisms (or fallacies) that it is impossible to tell a lie (284C), that Ctesippus' father is a dog (298E), and that if a man knows one thing, he knows everything (294A). At *Euthydemus* 278B,

---

[18] Galen, *De Animi Peccatis Dignoscendis*, in *Scripta Minora*, ed. by J. Marquardt, Vol. I (Leipzig: Teubner, 1884), pp. 31-32.
[19] *Ibid.*, pp. 32-33.
[20] Eduard Zeller, *Outlines of the History of Greek Philosophy*, rev. by W. Nestle and trans. by L. Palmer, Meridian Books (13th ed.; Cleveland: World Publishing Co., 1969), p. 297.
[21] Prantl, p. 559. Though Prantl classifies Galen as a Later Peripatetic in logic, he notices that Galen is in general known as an Eclectic philosopher.
[22] Galen, *De Placitis Hippocratis et Platonis*, ed. by Iwan Müller (Leipzig: Teubner, 1874). In this treatise Galen argues against the Stoics that the tripartite soul—intellect, spirit, and appetite—is located respectively in the brain, the heart, and the liver, and furthermore, he claims that Plato and Hippocrates agree with him.

through the mouth of Socrates, Plato identifies one source of sophisms as being ambiguity (ἡ τῶν ὀνομάτων διαφορά), which is the subject that occupies most of Galen's attention in *De Captionibus*.

Aristotle's *Sophistici Elenchi*, on the other hand, provides rules for the production and identification of sophisms. With regard to its relationship to the *Euthydemus*, Kneale and Kneale state that it resembles Plato's dialogue ('from which about a tenth of its examples could have been drawn') in that the majority of the examples are both fallacious and trivial in content.[23] The only serious examples in the *Sophistici Elenchi* are mathematical (squaring the circle)[24] and metaphysical (the Third Man).[25]

With respect to the sillier sophisms, E. Kapp's view seems correct—that they had become 'syllogistical games' that were played as mental exercises by beginners in philosophy.[26] Their ridiculous content had two primary virtues; to wit, it made such exercises enjoyable and amusing for the participants,[27] and it was no threat to the established doctrines of the school.[28]

Though there is evidence that certain sophisms were used in debate in the laws courts of antiquity,[29] there is reason to believe that these arguments also had a purely theoretical use. Along these lines, Kneale and Kneale suggest that certain teachers of sophistry studied sophisms for the purpose of formulating principles of logic.[30] Such principles might be formal or otherwise, depending on the method or interests of the investigator. And it seems reasonable to believe that it was an enterprise of this nature that occupied Galen's attention (at least partially) in *De Captionibus*.

We might well wonder why Galen undertook to write this introductory treatise on sophisms due to language. One obvious motivating factor is Galen's commitment as a teacher. Galen seems to imply in one passage that he held classes in the recognition of valid arguments and that by learning to identify valid arguments,

---

[23] Kneale and Kneale, p. 13.
[24] Aristotle *De Sophisticis Elenchis* 11. 171ᵇ12-18, and Kneale and Kneale, p. 13.
[25] *Soph. El.* 23. 178ᵇ36-39.
[26] Ernst Kapp, *Greek Foundations of Traditional Logic* (New York: Columbia University Press, 1942), p. 64.
[27] See Plato *Respublica* 7. 539B.
[28] Kapp, p. 64.
[29] For an example, see Aulus Gellius *Noctes Atticae* 5. 10. 405.
[30] Kneale and Kneale, p. 14.

his students could immediately detect sophisms when proposed to them.[31] In *De Captionibus* Galen makes use of the opposite method for the instruction of beginners—teaching the recognition of (and principles behind) certain invalid arguments.

A more general motive for Galen's writing this treatise and a more impelling reason for his great interest in sophisms becomes clear from a further look at Galen as a physician-philosopher. As the outstanding logician and scientist of his day, Galen undertakes to refute opinions of his physician colleagues whom he often refers to as sophists,[32] and correlatively to demonstrate his own findings.[33] As N. Gilbert has expressed it,

> Throughout his life he [Galen] held to a strict ideal of scientific proof and campaigned against the lax methods of his fellow physicians, who were inclined to accept received views without seeking a sound basis for them in experience or logic. He insisted that the characteristic of the doctor who seeks to achieve a firm grasp of the principles of his craft must be, not respect for the opinions of Plato or Aristotle or anyone else, but only regard for the truth.[34]

Proceeding in accordance with Galen's principles requires adherence to method. An essential component of this method is the avoidance of ambiguity in language.

In a passage referred to and translated by Gilbert,[35] Galen writes that the investigator who uses demonstrations must take account of both things and their names. In addition he must learn to distinguish differences in words from differences in the things they signify. Galen's method to mark these distinctions is twofold—first, to begin with the differences in things alone, making certain by demonstration that the problem at hand is concerned with these things solely, and second, to pursue the discussion in accordance with each separate name assigned to

---

[31] Galen, *De Animi Peccatis Dignoscendis* (*Scripta Minora*) Vol. II, p. 57. In this work Galen describes sophisms as false arguments which through adulteration resemble true arguments (p. 56).

[32] An example may be found in Galen's *On the Natural Faculties*, trans. by A. J. Brock, Loeb Classical Library (Cambridge, Mass.: Harvard University Press, 1916), 1.13, (p. 55).

[33] For an example, see *ibid.*, 3.1. (p. 225).

[34] Gilbert, p. 14.

[35] *Ibid.*, p. 20.

each separate thing, without changing the meaning of a word in any way but preserving it as it was fixed at the beginning.[36]

These preliminary remarks should suffice to make clear where the question of ambiguity in language enters Galen's discussion of method; namely, at rock bottom. The absence of ambiguity is a basic requirement for all scientific discourse. Ambiguity must be avoided by the competent investigator at all costs and if it is used by another in argument, it must be detected and exposed for immediate refutation of a false or unwarranted opinion. In this light one easily recognizes the utility Galen must have intended for *De Captionibus* as a training manual for philosophers and physicians.

---

[36] Galen, *De Methodo Medendi* (Kühn ed.) Vol. X, pp. 44-45. Some of the ideas here seem to be a legacy of Plato's *Cratylus* (387D-388B).

CHAPTER TWO

THE CONCEPT OF AMBIGUITY AND ITS RELATION TO THE STUDY OF FALLACY

In this chapter I describe the general concept of ambiguity and show its relation to the study of fallacy. The Greek inquiry into these topics is set in more general perspective when located within the conceptual framework that is proposed here.

As a purely descriptive feature of language, ambiguity is properly analyzed by the linguist or philosopher of language. Ambiguity has many uses, however, and depending on its context, may be deemed to be either a desirable or undesirable linguistic phenomenon.

When skillfully employed in literature, for example, ambiguity may be highly desirable. There its use is encouraged when it enhances the effectiveness of a poem or prose work, as when its presence contributes to the intended production of humor.[1] Consider the passage in *Alice in Wonderland* in which Alice and the others are drenched in the pool of tears and the Mouse promises to make them dry, stating, 'This is the driest thing I know,' and then proceeds to recite a tedious excerpt from a British history book![2]

Furthermore, the use of metaphor introduces ambiguity into language, which scientific and philosophical discourse could scarcely do without. For example, some theorists characterize a covering law or scientific nomic generalization as an *instrument* for predicting future events, and some mathematicians, without incoherence, call a number a *point* on a line.

On the other hand, ambiguity is undesirable in discourse when it tends to cause misunderstanding. Specifically, in logical argument

---

[1] Max Black, in *The Labyrinth of Language*, Mentor Books (New York and Toronto: New American Library, 1968), p. 157, n. 1, observes, 'Poets as well as punsters, often get their best effects by meaning more than one thing at the same time ... these depend upon the schooled hearer or reader perceiving both meanings at once, not in order to hesitate between them, but rather in order to appreciate their relation and interplay.'
[2] Lewis Carroll, *The Annotated Alice: Alice's Adventures in Wonderland and Through the Looking Glass*, ed. by Martin Gardner, Forum Books (New York: World Publishing Co., 1963), p. 46.

ambiguity may be said to rate high negative value, for an inference made on the basis of an ambiguous premise may be invalid.

The present discussion will begin by delimiting the concept of ambiguity through negative characterization. Then definitions of ambiguity will be offered.

First of all, ambiguity is not vagueness. A word is vague when there is a large area of uncertainty as to its application.[3] For example, the general term 'middle-aged' is vague because the borderline of its applicability is wide. It means 'of the time of life between youth and old age,' but it is unclear whether 'middle-aged' applies (or is true of) a thirty year old or a thirty-five year old.[4]

Moreover, ambiguity is not multiple applicability either in the trivial or non-trivial sense. Trivially, every general term (or count noun) is multiply applicable in that it may be true of, or truly predicated of, more than one thing. For example, 'man' is true of both Chrysippus and Galen. Non-trivially, a term is multiply applicable by virtue of applying to more than one *kind* of thing. An example from Aristotle is 'contingent,' which is said to apply to three kinds of thing—what is necessary, not necessary, and possible.[5] But 'contingent' does not *mean* these three things, and hence is not a case of ambiguity.[6]

---

[3] On the subject of vagueness, see William P. Alston, *Philosophy of Language* (Englewood Cliffs: Prentice-Hall, Inc., 1964), pp. 84-90. On vagueness, W. V. O. Quine, in *Word and Object* (Cambridge, Mass.: M.I.T. Press, 1960), p. 126, states: 'Commonly a general term true of physical objects will be vague in two ways: as to the several boundaries of all its objects and as to the inclusion or exclusion of marginal objects. Thus take the general term 'mountain:' it is vague on the score of how much terrain to reckon into each of the indisputable mountains, and it is vague on the score of what lesser eminences to count as mountains at all.'

[4] Quine (*Word and Object*, p. 127) notices that vagueness is at times of value even to the philosopher. He writes that vagueness 'is an aid in coping with the linearity of discourse. An expositor finds that an understanding of some matter A is necessary preparation for an understanding of B, and yet that A cannot itself be expounded in correct detail without, conversely, noting certain exceptions and distinctions which require prior understanding of B. Vagueness, then, to the rescue. The expositor states A vaguely, proceeds to B, and afterward touches up A, without ever having to call upon his reader to learn and unlearn any outright falsehood in the preliminary statement of A.'

[5] *Analytica Priora* I. 3. 25^{a}37-39.

[6] In the *Soph. El.* one is tempted to believe that Aristotle is not quite straight on the notions of ambiguity and multiple applicability, (both of which he calls 'πολλαχῶς λεγόμενα'). For there he introduces the study

Finally, ambiguity is not indeterminacy of speech act. That is, a sentence is not ambiguous because its utterance may count as the performance of two or more speech acts. For example, the sentence 'I am in pain' has only one sense (and one set of truth conditions), but it is unclear whether by uttering it I am making a complaint, expressing discomfort, or merely stating a matter of fact.

Now that several kinds of linguistic phenomena have been ruled out as being ambiguity, the next question to decide is what it is that is ambiguous. It has been suggested that ambiguity is a function not of words and sentences but rather of particular utterances, the datable uses of words and sentences.[7] That is, though 'pen' as a word has two meanings, 'animal enclosure' and 'writing instrument,' the datable *use* of the sentence 'The pen is quite large' (by someone entering a farm yard) is unambiguous. Although neither Aristotle nor Galen explicitly distinguishes the ambiguity of a word or sentence in a datable context, each does presuppose (and so does the present discussion) that ambiguity is primarily a property of sentences *and* that the ambiguity of these sentences is left unresolved by the contexts in which they occur.[8]

---

of sophistical refutations by reference to the fact that the same sentence or word signifies more than one way because the number of words and sentences is finite, though the number of things (πράγματα) is infinite (*Soph. El.* 1. 165ª10-13). But aside from this remark, Aristotle's discussion thereafter in the *Soph. El.* concerns ambiguity and not multiple applicability of general terms. It may be noted that Aristotle refers to ambiguity by the expressions 'διττόν,' 'πολλαχῶς λεγόμενα,' and 'σημαίνειν πλείω' indifferently (*Soph. El.* 19. 177ª9-12).

[7] On this topic, see G.E.L. Owen, 'Aristotle on the Snares of Ontology,' in *New Essays on Plato and Aristotle*, ed. by Renford Bambrough (London: Routledge & Kegan Paul, 1965), pp. 74-75. Owen claims to draw his inspiration from P. F. Strawson, presumably in his article 'On Referring,' *Mind*, LIX (July, 1950).

[8] A worthwile discussion of the Greek and particularly Aristotle's notion of a sentence is Jaakko Hintikka's 'Time, Truth, and Knowledge in Ancient Greek Philosophy,' *American Philosophical Quarterly*, IV (January, 1967), 2-4. Hintikka instructively writes: '... for Aristotle the typical sentences used in expressing human knowledge or opinion are not among those Quine calls *eternal sentences* (or, even among *standing sentences*) but among those Quine calls *occasion sentences*. That is to say, they are not sentences to which we assent or from which we dissent once and for all. They are sentences to which we can subscribe or with which we must disagree on the basis of some feature or features of the occasion on which they are uttered (or written). In particular the sentences Aristotle is apt to have in mind

At any rate, Aristotle, Galen, and the present discussion assume that the word is the minimal unit of ambiguous discourse. The following purports to be a general definition (in terms of necessary and sufficient conditions) of what is ordinarily called homonymy,[9] the clearest case of lexical ambiguity. The reliance of this definition on the notion of linguistic paraphrase obviates any commitment to meanings over and above those expressible by paraphrase values:[10]

> a word w is homonymous if and only if w admits of (at least) two paraphrases, x and y, and x and y are not paraphrases of one another

Paraphrases for a word w may be specified as answers to the question, 'what does w mean?' As an example of a homonym, consider 'light.' It is ambiguous because it admits of two paraphrases, 'having little weight for its size' and 'pale in color,' which are not paraphrases of one another. Clearly, in the case of homonymy the paraphrase relation *fails* to have the Euclidean property, which may be diagramed as follows ('⟶' being read 'is paraphrased by'):

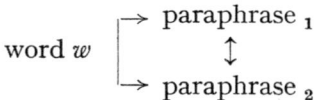

In the case of univocity, on the other hand, the paraphrase relation has the Euclidean property; for all the paraphrases of a univocal word are paraphrases of each other.

The paraphrase relation is both symmetrical and nonreflexive. It is symmetrical in that an expression, e.g., 'light' and its paraphrase 'pale in color' are paraphrases of one another. It is nonreflexive because an expression, e.g., 'light' is not a paraphrase

---

are *temporally indefinite*; they depend on the time of their utterance.... Aristotle would apparently have accepted the doctrine that the sentence 'It is raining' is made true or false by different sets of facts accordingly as it is uttered today or yesterday.'

[9] Henceforth, two words will be said to be homonyms if they have different paraphrase values, but are formally indistinguishable both orthographically and phonologically, their etymological careers, whether the same or different, being counted as irrelevant.

[10] The notion of paraphrase value (although extended here) derives from the analysis of Irena Bellert and Henry Hiż, in 'Paraphrastic Sets and Grammatical Analysis, Part 1,' *University of Pennsylvania Transformations and Discourse Analysis Papers*, No. 59 (1965).

of itself. A paraphrase by its very nature must be a rewording of that which is to be paraphrased.

It may be noted that the above definition of homonymy is specified independently of the semantic notion of truth. One might take Quine's tack [11] and describe an ambiguous word as one which may be both true and false of the same thing. For example, 'light' may be true and false of a black feather. But it seems reasonable to suppose that this characterization of lexical ambiguity by reference to truth and falsity reflects, in terms of truth conditions which may differ, the difference in paraphrase value of an ambiguous general term.

As was suggested above, ambiguity is primarily a function of sentences, whether it occurs in literature, the sciences, or in logic. Hence our discussion will focus on the formulation of a definition of *sentential* ambiguity. Such a definition resembles our definition of lexical ambiguity by its reference to paraphrase values: [12]

> a sentence[13] s is ambiguous if and only if s admits of (at least) two paraphrases, t and u, and t and u are not paraphrases of one another.

All ambiguous sentences, not only those whose ambiguity is due to their grammatical or syntactic structure [14] conform to this

---

[11] Quine, (*Word and Object*), p. 131.

[12] The relation of sentential paraphrases is symmetrical and nonreflexive like the relation of lexical paraphrases. The rewording of a sentence need not effect every word in it. Some words, e.g., proper names, that occur in a sentence may occur also in the paraphrase of that sentence.

[13] Included as a 'sentence' in this definition of sentential ambiguity are also clauses and phrases. See *infra* p. 13. n.14.

[14] The definitions of sentential ambiguity offered by exponents of constituent-structure and transformational grammar are in fact definitions of a species of sentential ambiguity; namely, grammatical or syntactic ambiguity. Such ambiguity arises from the disposition of a constituent (or constituents) in a sentence to play more than one grammatical role. According to John Lyons, in *Introduction to Theoretical Linguistics* (Cambridge: Cambridge University Press, 1968), pp. 211-15, a constituent-structure analyst might define grammatical ambiguity as follows: a sentence (or phrase) is ambiguous if its non-linear constituent-structure may be resolved in more than one way. For example, the noun-phrase 'new automobile shipment' may be specified as 'Adjective and ($Noun_1$ and $Noun_2$) or as '(Adjective and $Noun_1$) and $Noun_2$.' The parentheses indicate what is being construed with what in each resolution of the structure of the phrase in question.

For a transformationalist, on the other hand, a sentence is grammatically ambiguous if (at least) two deep structures correspond to its one surface definition. Hence, it includes sentences whose ambiguity is due to homonymy: e.g., 'The pen is constructed of metal,' which may be paraphrased as 'The small enclosure for animals is made of metal' and 'The writing instrument that uses ink is made of metal,' sentences which are not paraphrases of one another. An example of a sentence with syntactic ambiguity is 'The love of God is a pillar of the faith,' which may be paraphrased 'God's love for men is a pillar of the faith' and 'Man's love for God is a pillar of the faith.'

The definition above is designed to capture the general notion of ambiguity, in whatever sort of discourse it may occur. It might be objected that this definition is too narrow because it fails to include as cases of ambiguity examples that a literary critic like William Empson designates as such. But this may be countered by reference to Empson's own admission that he uses 'ambiguity' in an extended sense.[15] Empson counts as ambiguous those sentences with words that suggest various associations, or have different 'incidental connections of meaning,' which would not figure in the paraphrase value of these sentences (unless the notion of paraphrase value were also extended).

The logician, on the other hand, may wish to define sentential ambiguity in a way that makes plain his interest in the subject. He might do so by reference to the notion of entailment, formulating the conditions of sentential ambiguity as follows:

---

structure. Galen's example of amphiboly, (*De Captionibus* (Gabler ed.) p. 88 ll. 10-13, [henceforth, 88,10-13]), γένοιτο καταλαβεῖν τὸν ὗν ἐμέ, is a case of a sentence with a surface structure which neutralizes the distinct transitive sentences embedded in the indirect discourse construction. (This transformational analysis is based on Lyon's analysis of a Latin sentence with a similar surface structure, pp. 253-54). That is, either ἐγὼ κατέλαβον τὸν ὗν ('I caught the boar') or κατέλαβε ὁ ὗς ἐμέ ('The boar caught me') is embedded in the indirect discourse construction καταλαβεῖν τὸν ὗν ἐμέ, in which both 'the boar' and 'me' are in the accusative, and each of these nouns can function as either subject or object of καταλαβεῖν.

[15] William Empson, *Seven Types of Ambiguity* (3rd ed.; New York: New Directions Publishing Corp., 1966), p. 1. Here Empson writes, 'An ambiguity, in ordinary speech, means something very pronounced, and as a rule witty or deceitful. I propose to use the word in an extended sense, and shall think relevant to my subject any verbal nuance, however slight, which gives room for alternative reactions to the same piece of language. Sometimes ... the word may be stretched absurdly far, but it is descriptive because it suggests the analytical mode of approach, and with that I am concerned.'

> a sentence s is ambiguous if and only if s admits paraphrases t and u, at least one of which does not entail the other.[16]

Although this definition is elegant, it does not reflect as plainly as the following definition (of the same notion) the connection between an ambiguous sentence, entailment, and fallacy:

> a sentence s is ambiguous if and only if s admits paraphrases t and u, such that the conjunction of t with another sentence v, entails some p, and the conjunction of u with v fails to entail that p.

For example, consider as s, 'Marblehill is a wealthy girls' school.' It may be paraphrased as t, 'Marblehill is a wealthy school for girls,' and as u, 'Marblehill is a school for wealthy girls.' According to the first proposed definition of sentential ambiguity, s is ambiguous because of its paraphrases t and u, neither entails the other.

To illustrate that s is ambiguous according to the second proposed definition, another sentence (premise) must be introduced, v. If we assume that v is 'Each wealthy school for girls has a large endowment,' then the conjunction of t and v entails p, 'Marblehill has a large endowment,' but the conjunction of u and v fails to entail p, and hence s is ambiguous. Even if both u and v were true, it is possible for p to be false, and hence p is not entailed by their conjunction.

The leads to the next point—that the sentences into which an ambiguous sentence may be paraphrased need not differ in truth value. It is the case only that no logical contradiction results if it turns out that the paraphrase sentences do differ in truth value.[17] Clearly, that Marblehill is a school for wealthy girls is consistent with Marblehill's not being a wealthy school for girls.

---

[16] I owe this formulation to Professor Brian Chellas.

[17] Aristotle states at *Soph. El.* 19. 177ª14-15, 'That which is ambiguous is now true and now false, and what is ambiguous signifies that which is the case and that which is not the case,' (my translation). Presumably Aristotle is here indicating a mark of linguistic ambiguity; namely, that an ambiguous sentence admits of distinct truth values. He most likely has in mind a sentence like 'Speaking of the silent is possible' (which is mentioned just two lines earlier in this passage), which on one reading is true, 'It is possible that the things spoken of are silent' and on another is false, 'It is possible for one speaking, when he speaks, to be silent.' (These two paraphrases may be found at *Soph. El.* 4. 166ª12-14). Aristotle here seems to overlook the point that it is possible for both readings of an ambiguous

Precisely what is the logician's interest in ambiguity? First and foremost, it is to decrease the amount of its occurrence both in his own discourse and in that of others. For ambiguity not only creates uncertainty as to the exact basis for an inference (when it affects a premise), but also causes fallacies. A fallacy due to ambiguity results when a premise is accepted in one sense, and a conclusion is illicitly drawn on the basis of that same premise taken in a different sense. And it may be noted that this invalid inference may be intentional (in the case of the sophist) or inadvertent.

What motivates the philosopher or logician to reflect on the nature of ambiguity is his desire to be able to recognize and avoid its occurrence in his own reasoning [18] (and of course, to detect it in the discourse of others). It is no wonder that a theory of ambiguity is born within the context of the study of fallacy. The history of philosophy bears witness to the fact that the pioneers in the investigation of ambiguity were pioneers in the investigation of fallacy. And although their concern was with ambiguity as an undesirable phenomenon in language, their theoretical descriptions of ambiguity are achievements in general linguistics.

---

sentence to be true. In any case, Aristotle asserts at *Categoriae* 5. 4^{a}36-4^{b}1, that an unambiguous sentence like 'A particular man is sitting' is sometimes true and sometimes false, depending on whether the subject in question is sitting or standing. For more discussion of this passage, see Hintikka, in 'Time, Truth, and Knowledge,' pp. 2-4.

[18] See Aristotle *Ars Rhetorica* 1. 3.

CHAPTER THREE

ARISTOTLE ON FALLACY AND AMBIGUITY

Galen's *De Captionibus* may be seen as a legacy of Aristotelian inquiry into fallacy and ambiguity in language, and here I sketch Aristotle's contribution in these areas. Though Galen is writing nearly five centuries after Aristotle, he treats the topic of ambiguity as if Aristotle were the only previous contributor worth taking seriously. This fact explains in part why *De Captionibus* is in form a kind of commentary on the *Sophistici Elenchi* but is in content a treatise on the correct use and abuse of language. In any case, by distinguishing the Aristotelian doctrine we may better appreciate Galen's own achievement—the formulation of a comprehensive theory of ambiguity.

We find that Aristotle has no general systematic teaching on ambiguity outside the context of his theory of fallacy but that he does have a special doctrine of ambiguity, 'focal meaning,'[1] which has crucial implications with regard to the possibility of a science of metaphysics. Although this latter doctrine seems to play no part in Galen's work on ambiguity, I adumbrate it here as part of the Aristotelian teaching on ambiguity to which Galen had access.

One of the marks of the Aristotelian general doctrine of ambiguity is its lack of rigor, presumably the result of an absence of a theoretical foundation. This is clearly emphasized in contrast with Galen's teaching on ambiguity, which is imbued with a rigid theoretical framework. At any rate, Aristotle requests that the reader pardon the shortcomings of his treatment of reasoning [2] (including fallacy and ambiguity), claiming that his own work is the first to be written on the subject. I shall proceed first to discuss Aristotle's general teaching on fallacy and ambiguity, and afterward turn to his special theory.

Aristotle's doctrine on fallacy and ambiguity is preserved in his treatise *Sophistici Elenchi*, which is considered an appendix

---

[1] See *infra* pp. 29-31.
[2] *Soph. El.* 34. 184^{b}1-8.

to his *Topica*,³ a handbook on reasoning from dialectical premises.⁴ According to Ryle this exercise in dialectic is a formal debate, in which one participant is questioner, the other, answerer.⁵ In these eristic moots,

> The questioner can only ask questions; and the answerer can, with certain qualifications, answer only 'yes' or 'no'. . . . The questioner has to try to extract from the answer, by a series of questions, an answer or conjunction of answers inconsistent with the original thesis, i.e. drive him into an 'elenchus.' The questioner has won the duel if he succeeds in getting the answerer to contradict his original thesis, or else in forcing him to resign, or in reducing him to silence, to an infinite regress, to mere abusiveness, to pointless yammering or to outrageous paradox. The answerer has won if he succeeds in keeping his wicket up. . . . The answerer is allowed to object to a question on the score that, for example it is two or more questions in one, like *have you left off beating your father?*, or that it is metaphorical or ambiguous.⁶

As Ryle suggests and Aristotle asserts, to drive an opponent into self-refutation (i.e., reasoning which contradicts a given conclusion) ⁷ is only one aim in such contests.⁸ Nevertheless, Aristotle's description and solution of the sophistical refutations take up the bulk of the discussion in the *Sophistici Elenchi*.⁹ Aristotle characterizes sophistical refutations as refutations which appear to be genuine, but which are not, or as refutations which though genuine with respect to refuting some thesis, only appear to refute the thesis at hand.¹⁰ For Aristotle, fallacies ¹¹ (sophisms)

---

³ David Ross, *Aristotle*, University Paperbacks (London and New York: Methuen & Co., 1964), p. 59. In *Organon*, ed. by T. Waitz, Vol. II (Leipzig: Hahn, 1846), the *Sophistici Elenchi* forms Book Iota (IX) of the *Topica*. See Waitz, pp. 528-29.
⁴ Aristotle *Topica* 1. 1. 100ᵃ18-20.
⁵ Gilbert Ryle, 'Dialectic in the Academy,' in *New Essays on Plato and Aristotle* (ed. by R. Bambrough), p. 40.
⁶ *Ibid*.
⁷ *Soph. El.* 1. 165ᵃ2-3.
⁸ Four other goals are specified by Aristotle—forcing an opponent into falsehood, paradox, solecism and babbling. See *Soph. El.* 3. 165ᵇ13-22.
⁹ Chapters 4-11, 19-30.
¹⁰ *Soph. El.* 8. 169ᵇ20-23.
¹¹ At *Soph. El.* 4. 166ᵇ21, 28, Aristotle calls them paralogisms. At *Top.* 8. 12. 162ᵇ12 Aristotle includes arguments with false premises in the class of false (fallacious) arguments. Such arguments are of minimal interest to Aristotle in *Soph. El.*, where he focuses on invalid and spurious arguments, the premises of which may very well be true.

and sophistical refutations as *types* of apparent forms of reasoning, coincide. Hence, here my practice is to use the terms interchangeably.

Aristotle divides the fallacies into two classes, those due to language (*in dictione*, παρὰ τὴν λέξιν) and those independent of language (*extra dictionem*, ἔξω τῆς λέξεως).[12] The six fallacies of the first class are caused either by ambiguity in language or by linguistic confusion,[13] whereas those of the second class are not. Specified as such, those *extra dictionem* are only negatively characterized by Aristotle. They are seven in number and display great diversity. For example, among them is the fallacy of the Consequent, which according to Ryle, is the sole logical or formal fallacy 'about which Aristotle is perfectly clear in *De Sophisticis Elenchis.*'[14] The fallacy of the Consequent occurs of course, when it is supposed that the conditional (i.e., $p \supset q$) is convertible.[15] For example, 'If a man has a fever, then he is hot. Hence, if a man is hot, then he has a fever.'[16]

At the same time, the class of fallacies *extra dictionem* contains the fallacy Ignoratio Elenchi, which occurs when a given refutation fails to conform with the definition of a refutation, and hence does not contradict the thesis to be refuted, though it appears to do so.[17] The example Aristotle gives is a sophistical refutation of the thesis 'Two is not both double and not double (the same number)':

(1) Two is the double of one.
(2) Two is not the double of three.
∴ (3) Two is both double and not double.[18]

Clearly the above fails to contradict the original thesis, though it may appear to, and hence is a case of Ignoratio Elenchi. But this fallacy does not seem to be a specific one, coordinate with

---

[12] *Soph. El.* 4. 165ᵇ23-24.
[13] By linguistic confusion, I mean the taking of one word or sentence for another; that is, the confusing of one word or sentence with another word or sentence.
[14] Ryle, p. 65.
[15] *Soph. El.* 5. 167ᵇ1-2.
[16] *Soph. El.* 5. 167ᵇ18-20.
[17] *Soph. El.* 5. 167ᵃ21-23. It arises from ignorance of the notion of a refutation and is also called defect of definition (ἡ ἔλλειψις τοῦ λόγου) of a refutation.
[18] *Soph. El.* 5. 167ᵃ29-30.

Accident,[19] Secundum Quid,[20] Many Questions,[21] False Cause,[22] Petitio Principii, [23] the Consequent, and the six fallacies *in dictione*. Rather it appears to be a generic fallacy under which the rest of the fallacies fall. And in a passage of reflective self-criticism Aristotle admits that it is possible to analyze all the fallacies he specifies as cases of Ignoratio Elenchi.[24] Hence, Aristotle himself identifies and thereby acknowledges imprecision in his classification. That all the fallacies fall under one, however, is a claim independent of Aristotle's observation that a given argument may have more than one flaw [25] and may consequently be a case of more than one fallacy. For example, he notices that the above example of Ignoratio Elenchi may also be considered a case of one of the fallacies *in dictione* (presumably Homonymy),[26] and that a case of Accident like 'The dog is yours. The dog is a father. Thus the dog is your father,' may be held to be a case of ambiguity,[27] and thus, of some fallacy *in dictione*.

Since the six fallacies *in dictione* are caused and denominated

---

[19] The fallacy Accident occurs when it is assumed that some attribute belongs to and is predicable of both a thing and its accident (*Soph. El.* 5. 166^{b}28-30). E.g., 'The dog is yours. The dog is a father. Thus, the dog is your father.' (*Soph. El.* 24. 179^{a}34-35, 179^{b}14-15.)

[20] The fallacy Secundum Quid occurs when in at least one of the premises of an argument something is predicated only in part which is taken as though it were predicated without qualification (*Soph. El.* 5. 166^{b}37-167^{a}1). E.g., 'The Ethiopian is black. The Ethiopian has white teeth. Thus, the Ethiopian is both black and not black.' (*Soph. El.* 5. 167^{a}11-13.)

[21] The fallacy Many Questions occurs when one of the questions assented to (i.e., one of the premises) is really two but is treated as though it were singular (*Soph. El.* 5. 167^{b}38-168^{a}1). E.g., in the argument ' "Is a man" is true of A and B. Thus, if someone strikes A and B, he strikes a man, not men,' the premise is a conjunction 'A is a man and B is a man' but it is treated as if it were an atomic sentence, since the predicate 'is a man' occurs only once. (*Soph. El.* 5. 168^{a}5-7.)

[22] The fallacy False Cause occurs when in an indirect proof, a *reductio ad impossibile*, a premise is denied that is not required for the generation of the contradiction. (*Soph. El.* 5. 167^{b}21-24.)

[23] The fallacy Petitio Principii (Begging the Question) arises in an argument in which the original point to be proved is assumed in proving that same point (*Soph. El.* 5. 167^{a}36-39). E.g., when one proves 'the diagonal is incommensurable with the side' by assuming 'the side is incommensurable with the diagonal,' (*Top.* 8. 13. 163^{a}11-13).

[24] *Soph. El.* 6. 168^{a}17-20.

[25] *Soph. El.* 24. 179^{b}17.

[26] *Soph. El.* 5. 167^{a}35.

[27] *Soph. El.* 24. 179^{b}38-180^{a}1. See *supra* p. 20, n. 19. The Stoics might take this fallacy to be a case of ambiguity. See *infra* pp. 62-63.

by the kinds of ambiguity and linguistic confusion that affect one of their premises or their conclusion, Aristotle's classification of these fallacies will be a classification of ambiguity in language and of linguistic confusion. The fallacies Homonymy, Amphiboly, and Form of expression [28] arise from double meaning (ambiguity), whereas the fallacies Combination, Division, and Accent arise not from ambiguity but from linguistic confusion, that is, from the taking of one word or sentence for another.

Galen, however, identifies Aristotle's fallacies *in dictione* as cases of ambiguity only, not of linguistic confusion,[29] and hence his reading of the *Sophistici Elenchi* is inaccurate. The discrepancy between what Aristotle's teaching is and what Galen says it is may be attributable to Galen's interest in a unified general account of ambiguity and his corresponding failure to appreciate the less than systematic nature of Aristotle's discussion. This misreading of Aristotle is reflected in Galen's own conception of the fallacies *in dictione* as being solely cases of ambiguity. Let us now turn to the individual Aristotelian fallacies *in dictione*, for they constitute Galen's point of departure in *De Captionibus*.[30]

The fallacy Homonymy arises when two conditions are met. First, one of the words that occurs in at least one of the premises of an argument or in the conclusion is homonymous; that is, has two senses, and causes the entire sentence to be ambiguous. Second, the inference made assumes that the sentence in question means one thing, whereas it is assented to as a premise as meaning something else. One of the examples Aristotle gives of this fallacy is as follows:

(1) The man who has recovered is healthy.
(2) The sick man has recovered.
∴ (3) The sick man is healthy.

---

[28] With their first letters capitalized Amphiboly, Homonymy, and Form of expression refer to kinds of fallacies in this section on Aristotle. Uncapitalized, amphiboly, homonymy, and form of expression refer to the modes of ambiguity which cause and denominate the corresponding fallacy.

[29] See Gabler's edition of *De Captionibus*, infra p., 92, lines 8-11, (henceforth, 92,8-11). H.W.B. Joseph commits this same error in expounding Aristotle on fallacies in *An Introduction to Logic* (Oxford: Clarendon Press, 1906), p. 538.

[30] The order in which these six fallacies are discussed here diverges from Aristotle's own, which is Homonymy, Amphiboly, Combination, Division, Accent, and Form of expression. I take the three genuine cases of ambiguity first, and then discuss the three cases of linguistic confusion.

(4) The sick man is sick.
∴ (5) The sick man (κάμνων) is both sick and healthy.[31]

Aristotle points out that 'sick man' ('κάμνων') means both 'a man who is currently sick' and 'a man who was sick in the past.'[32] In the above argument, presumably 'sick man' has the first sense in (4) and (5), but the second sense in (2) and (3)—otherwise no one would assent to (2) and hence (3) could not be inferred. The inference to (5) is made as though 'sick man' were univocal in all of its occurrences in the argument, which it is not.

It may be noted that Aristotle's notion of an homonymous word as one with (at least) two different definitions seems to coincide with his notion of homonymy in the *Categoriae*. Strictly speaking, however, there the things signified rather than their common name are said to be homonymous.[33]

The fallacy Amphiboly occurs when one of the constituent sentences of an argument is amphibolous, *and* when the inference made assumes that the sentence in question means one thing (is univocal) whereas it is assented to by the answerer as meaning something else. A sentence is amphibolous for Aristotle when its words are univocal taken in isolation, but are ambiguous taken together.[34] That is, amphiboly is not a question of one word with two senses, but of one sentence with an ambiguous syntactical structure; for example, the sentence 'I wish you the enemy may capture.' [35] In it none of the words is homonymous. The ambiguity arises from the fact that both 'you' and 'enemy' can assume more than one syntactic role; i.e., each may be construed either as the subject or as the object of 'may capture'.[36]

---

[31] *Soph. El.* 4. 165ᵇ38-166ᵃ6. This example turns on a feature of Greek that is not reflected in the translation. This case of Homonymy arises because the present participle in Greek also serves as the participle of the finite verb in the imperfect.

[32] *Soph. El.* 4. 166ᵃ2-4.

[33] *Cat.* 1. 1ᵃ1-3. In the *Soph. El.*, the *word* is normally the homonym. See e.g., *Soph. El.* 4. 165ᵇ29-35.

[34] *Soph. El.* 4. 166ᵃ17-18.

[35] *Soph. El.* 4. 166ᵃ6-7.

[36] The above grammatical description is more Stoic and contemporary than Aristotelian. Although it is clear that Aristotle recognizes (albeit dimly) the notion of structural ambiguity, he lacks the technical terminology to express it more precisely than by saying that this sort of ambiguity arises from the combining of words that are univocal in isolation (*Soph. El.* 4. 166ᵃ17-18).

One of Aristotle's examples of the fallacy Amphiboly is:

(1) You insist on being what you insist on being.
(2) You insist on a stone being.
∴ (3) You insist on being a stone.[37]

Here one assents to (2) as meaning 'You insist that a stone exists,' construing 'stone' as the subject of 'being.' But the inference that is made illicitly assumes that (2) means 'You insist that you are a stone,' construing 'stone' as the predicate nominative with 'being.'

The fallacy Form of expression occurs when one of the constituent words or sentences of an argument is ambiguous owing to its form of expression, *and* when the inference made assumes that the word or sentence in question has the sense which its form of expression suggests. A word or sentence [38] is ambiguous due to form of expression when the form in which it is expressed is similar to the form of another expression, and it is supposed that because of this formal similarity, they are similar in significance. For Aristotle the difference in significance of two expressions which their form of expression disguises is specified by a difference in logic. That is, because of their likeness of form, such expressions are thought to have a similar logic, whereas in fact, they belong to different logical categories. As Aristotle points out, the meanings of the two expressions only *appear* to be similar by virtue of the language in which they are expressed.[39] Nevertheless, for the one who is so deceived by appearances, the word or sentence does have a double meaning.[40]

One of Aristotle's examples of the fallacy Form of expression is as follows:

(1) 'He is cut,' 'he is burnt,' 'he is affected by a sensible object' are similar expressions and all signify passivities.
(2) Running, and telling are activities, and seeing is

---

[37] *Soph. El.* 4. 166ᵃ10-12, (adaptation of Loeb translation). In Greek the fallacy arises from the ambiguity of the second premise, which has an indirect discourse construction. The ambiguity results from the disposition of 'λίθον' ('stone') in the accusative case, to function as either subject of or predicate with the infinitive 'εἶναι'.

[38] Aristotle seems indifferent as to whether form of expression applies to single terms or complexes of them. See *Soph. El.* 22.

[39] *Soph. El.* 22. 178ᵃ23-24. Galen seizes upon this use of 'appear' in his own theory.

[40] *Soph. El.* 6. 168ᵃ23-25.

        expressed in a form similar to that in which they are expressed.
      (3) Seeing is a way of being affected by a sensible object.
∴ (4) Seeing is both an activity and a passivity.[41]

Although one might grant that all the premises in the above are true, the argument is a case of the fallacy Form of expression: clearly, the inference of (4) presupposes that 'seeing' signifies and specifies the logical category 'activity' in (2), by virtue of the form in which it is expressed (namely, as an active participle).[42]

At this juncture I turn to those fallacies *in dictione* which arise from linguistic confusion. The fallacy Combination occurs when in an argument a premise p with the words divided in a certain way is assented to, but is confused with another premise p' which is combined in a different way, and the inference is invalidly drawn on the basis of p'. Aristotle provides the following example of Combination:

      (1) It is true to say at the present moment, you are born.
∴ (2) You are born at the present moment.[43]

In this example, (1) is assented to with 'at the present moment' divided from 'you are born'—it is written with a comma after 'moment' and spoken with a pause after 'moment.' However, (1) is confused with another premise (sentence), (1'), 'It is true to say, at the present moment you are born,' which combines (or construes) 'at the present moment' with 'you are born.' And it is from this other sentence, (1') that (2) is inferred. Clearly, (2) does *not* follow from (1) as stated.

The fallacy Division is the converse of the fallacy Combination.[44]

---

[41] *Soph. El.* 22. 178ᵃ11-16.

[42] Although it does not turn on an ambiguity of the logical category being specified, a famous nineteenth century example of a fallacy arising from form of expression appears in J. S. Mill, *Utilitarianism*, ed. by O. Piest (2nd rev. ed.; New York: Library of Liberal Arts Press, 1957), p. 44: 'The only proof capable of being given that an object is visible is that people actually see it. The only proof that a sound is audible is that people hear it; and so of the other sources of our experience. In like manner, I apprehend, the sole evidence it is possible to produce that anything is desirable is that people do actually desire it.'

[43] *Soph. El.* 20. 177ᵇ20-22. This is a clear example of a fallacy that is non-syllogistic.

[44] These fallacies arise according to Aristotle, 'because we suppose that it makes no difference whether the phrase be combined or divided, as is indeed the case with most phrases,' (Oxford translation, *Soph. El.* 7. 169ᵃ25-27).

Division arises when in an argument a premise p with the words combined in a certain way is assented to, but is confused with another premise p' which is divided in a different way, and the inference is invalidly drawn on the basis of p'. For example,

(1) 5 is 2 and 3.
∴ (2) 5 is even and odd.[45]

In the above, (1) is assented to as combined; that is, '2' and '3' together are predicated of 5. But (1) is confused with the following premise (1'), '5 is 2, and 3,' which may be paraphrased '5 is 2 and 5 is 3.' In (1') '2' and '3' separately (as divided) are predicated of 5. And it is on the basis of (1') and the premises, '2 is even' and '3 is odd' that (2) is illicitly inferred. Again, as in the case of Combination, the fallacy occurs not from sentential ambiguity but from linguistic confusion. But what is the evidence for and against this interpretation which is consistently absent from the commentaries [46] on the *Sophistici Elenchi*?

The prima facie evidence against my interpretation consists of statements by Aristotle which appear to suggest that in cases of Combination and Division, the fallacy depends on one sentence with two meanings; that is, on sentential ambiguity. For example, in indicating how to unravel these fallacies Aristotle states:

> ... if the expression (λόγος) means something different when divided and when combined, as soon as one's opponent draws his conclusion one should take the expression in the contrary way.[47]

And this suggests that the same expression (λόγος) has two meanings. Moreover, when he accounts for the fallacy Division, Aristotle states,

> For the same phrase (λόγος) would not be thought always to have the same meaning when divided and when combined ... .[48]

---

[45] *Soph. El.* 4. 166ª33-34.
[46] I am referring to Galen's *De Captionibus*, and Pseudo-Alexander's *In Aristotelis Sophisticos Elenchos Commentarium*. ed. by M. Wallies, (Berlin: *C.I.A.G.*, 1898), Vol. II, Pt. 3, p. 56, l. 27-p. 57, l. 3, which misreads *Soph. El.* 6. 168ª23-28 and follows Galen's analysis, at *Commentarius* p. 23, ll. 4-11. I am referring also to the account of Edward Poste in *Aristotle on Fallacies* (London: Macmillan and Co., 1866).
[47] *Soph. El.* 20. 177ª34-35 (Oxford translation).
[48] *Soph. El.* 4. 166ª35-36 (Oxford translation).

Here again Aristotle seems to be saying that the fallacy Division turns on the ambiguity of a single sentence, which may be construed in more than one way.

However, there is good reason to believe that Aristotle is speaking loosely in these two passages and that it is his imprecision that has misled the commentators. Aristotle's considered view of the matter seems to be reflected in the following statement,

> For of the fallacies connected with language, some are due to a double meaning, for example Homonymy, Amphiboly, and Similarity of form ... whereas Combination, Division, and Accent are due to the sentence not being the same or the word being different.[49]

That the fallacies Combination and Division are not cases of ambiguity for Aristotle is further supported by his assertion with regard to the fallacy Division,

> For what turns on division is not really ambiguous, (for the sentence when divided is not the same sentence) ...[50]

Aristotle's view seems to presuppose the following as a necessary condition of sentential [51] identity: sentence s is identical with sentence s' only if, when written, they have the same punctuation, and when spoken, the pauses are placed in the same places. Hence, in the example of Division above, the premise '5 is 2 and 3' is a sentence different from that with which it is confused, namely '5 is 2, and 3.' If Aristotle had held that '5 is 2 and 3' and '5 is 2, and 3' are the same sentence with a double meaning, then it seems that his fallacies Combination and Division would be cases of the fallacy Amphiboly. But what Aristotle is saying in his more precisely formulated description of these fallacies [52] is that Combination and Division differ from Amphiboly in that they depend on linguistic confusion (the confusing of one sentence for another), whereas Amphiboly depends on ambiguity.

The sixth Aristotelian fallacy *in dictione* is Accent, which seems to be the lexical counterpart of Combination and Division. The fallacy Accent arises when in an argument a premise p with the word w as constituent is assented to, but is confused with another

---

[49] *Soph. El.* 6. 168^{a}23-28 (adaptation of Loeb translation).
[50] *Soph. El.* 20. 177^{b}1-3 (adaptation of Loeb translation).
[51] Sentences here are sentence-types, not sentence-tokens.
[52] *Soph. El.* 20. 177^{a}38-177^{b}9.

premise (sentence) p' with the word w' substituted for w, w differs from w' solely by virtue of being accented [53] differently, and the inference is invalidly made on the basis of p' with w'. Aristotle observes that it is difficult to construct an argument of this type which is not written down.[54] It may be noted that in Aristotle's time, breathings and accents were not generally written; in fact, written accents had not yet been invented.[55] Aristotle also reports that only a few examples of the fallacy Accent occur in any form.[56] He offers the following as an illustration:

(1) οὗ καταλύεις (where you lodge) is a house.
(2) οὐ καταλύεις (you do not lodge) is a negation.
∴ (3) A house is a negation.[57]

In the above argument (1) is assented to with 'οὗ' as constituent of the sentence, but the inference is invalid, for it assumes that (1) is another sentence altogether, 'οὐ καταλύεις is a house,' which contains the word 'οὐ' instead of 'οὗ'. Hence in the fallacy Accent, one sentence is confused with another sentence, and this sentential confusion results from taking one word with certain accentuation for another word with different accentuation.[58] Hence, in Accent, the linguistic confusion is both sentential and lexical.

It seems reasonable to suppose that Aristotle's failure to countenance the fallacy Accent as a case of ambiguity may be credited to his linguistic intuitions on the matter. As examples of accent, he refers to the words 'ὅρος' (boundary) and 'ὄρος' (hill), and there seems no question that when they are pronounced according to their breathings and accentuation they are distinct.[59] When inscribed with their accentuation and breathing added, as 'ὅρος' and 'ὄρος', they also seem to be two words. The problem Aristotle faces by denying that Accent is a case of ambiguity is that the word for boundary and for hill can be written without any ac-

---

[53] Accentuation includes breathings for Aristotle. See *infra* p. 28, n. 60.
[54] *Soph. El.* 4. 166ᵇ1-2. In speech, the fallacy Accent occurs when 'the lowering or raising of the voice upon a phrase is thought not to alter its meaning . . . .' (*Soph. El.* 7. 169ᵃ27-29, Oxford translation).
[55] See *infra* p. 28 n. 60.
[56] *Soph. El.* 21. 177ᵇ35-37.
[57] *Soph. El.* 21. 177ᵇ37-178ᵃ2.
[58] Joseph (p. 542) observes that the fallacy Accent 'was perhaps distinguished from Equivocation [Homonymy], because words differently accented are not strictly the same word.'
[59] *Soph. El.* 22. 177ᵇ6-7. Clearly when spoken, different phonemes are uttered.

centuation or breathing, in *scriptura continua*,[60] as 'ορος'. In that case, 'ορος' meets Aristotle's criterion for lexical identity:

> In written language a word is the same when it is written with the same letters and in the same manner, though people now put in an additional sign . . .[61]

Hence, on the condition that 'ὅρος' and 'ὅρος' be written in *scriptura continua* as 'ορος', we have a case of double meaning.[62] But Aristotle does not reduce the fallacy Accent to the fallacy Homonymy, for at least in spoken language Accent may be viewed as a case of linguistic confusion, rather than of ambiguity.

Having considered Aristotle's teaching on fallacy, we find that not all fallacies are cases of ambiguity,[63] and that of the fallacies *in dictione* only three, Homonymy, Amphiboly, and Form of expression are cases of double meaning. Because of the imprecision that characterizes his descriptions of the fallacies, it is reasonable to believe that the *Sophistici Elenchi* represents an exploratory sketch made by Aristotle on the subject at hand. It may be noted that Aristotle does not irrevocably freeze the terminological usage that is developed in the *Sophistici Elenchi*.[64]

---

[60] A. N. Jannaris, in *An Historical Greek Grammar* (London: Macmillan and Co., 1897), p. 35, describes *scriptura continua* as the Greek method of writing all words in a continuous line. H. W. Smyth, in *Greek Grammar* (Cambridge, Mass: Harvard University Press, 1956), p. 38, sec. 161, states that the practice of placing accents was initiated by Aristophanes of Byzantium at the library of Alexandria c. 200 B.C. But signs for accents and breathings were not regularly employed in manuscripts until after 600 A.D. Sandys (*History of Classical Scholarship*, Vol. I, pp. 126-27) writes that these 'accents were invented with a view to preserving the true pronunciation, which was being corrupted by the mixed populations of the Greek world.' According to Sandys (p. 97), Aristotle recognizes a symbol for the rough breathing, by which the inscribed units ΟΡΟΣ (boundary) and ΟΡΟΣ (hill) are distinguished, and it is called a παράσημον (at *Soph. El.* 20. 177^{b}6). Sandys suggests that ΟΡΟΣ (boundary) was written ⊢ΟΡΟΣ.

[61] *Soph. El.* 20. 177^{b}4-6 (modified Loeb translation). By the expression 'in the same manner' Aristotle presumably means 'in the same order of sequence.'

[62] An analogous remark could be made about the fallacies Combination and Division when inscribed in *scriptura continua*.

[63] *Soph. El.* 20. 177^{b}7-10.

[64] For example, in his description of apparent enthymemes at *Rhet.* 2. 24. 1401^{a}1-8, Aristotle includes as a case of Form of expression one in which there is no ambiguity, but rather mere deception based on the form in which an apparent conclusion is expressed. He illustrates with the case of a rhetorician ending a discourse with a syllogistically expressed conclusion, 'Thus, so-and-so is such-and-such,' so as to make his hearers think he has drawn the conclusion of a syllogism, whereas he has provided no reasoning for this apparent conclusion.

Nevertheless, Aristotle's classification of fallacies and of ambiguity in language here does seem firmly grounded in strong philosophical and linguistic intuition. It is a mark of the seminal quality of his teaching on fallacy that its influence has been so pervasive in the history of philosophy from Galen to the present day.

I now turn to Aristotle's special doctrine of ambiguity, another section of the ancient philosophical landscape on the subject of double meaning. Aristotle's notion of focal meaning [65] or *pros hen* equivocity may be understood not as an outgrowth of the problem of fallacy but as a response to the problem of the possibility of the science of metaphysics, of being *qua* being, where 'being' is not univocal.

Just as homonymy is a species of ambiguity, so focal meaning is Aristotle's 'sophisticated variant on the idea of homonymy.' [66] We recall that in the *Eudemian Ethics* Aristotle argues that there is no science of being or of the good because 'being' and 'good' are ambiguous.[67] The presupposition of this argument is that if there is to be a science of metaphysics, of being *qua* being, (or of ethics), then 'being' (or 'good') must be univocal. But Aristotle wishes to make room for such a science, and in *Metaphysics* Γ 2, Z 4, and K 3 Aristotle relaxes this requirement of strict univocity. As he states,

> Since the science of the philosopher treats of being *qua* being universally and not in respect of a part of it, and 'being' has many senses and is not used in one only, it follows that if the word is used equivocally (ὁμωνύμως) and in virtue of nothing common to its various uses, being does not fall under one science (for the meanings of an equivocal term do not

---

[65] The name 'focal meaning' was coined for this special doctrine of Aristotle's by G. E. L. Owen, in 'Logic and Metaphysics in Some Earlier Works of Aristotle,' in *Aristotle and Plato in the Mid-Fourth Century*, ed. by I. Düring and G. E. L. Owen (Göteborg: Studia Graeca et Latina, 1960), p. 179. Focal meaning and its relation to Aristotle's overall teaching on ambiguity is an enormously complicated subject and deserves separate treatment. Here I only roughly sketch what I take to be Aristotle's doctrine.

[66] G. E. L. Owen, 'Aristotle on the Snares of Ontology,' in *New Essays on Plato and Aristotle* (ed. by R. Bambrough), pp. 72-73. Also on this and related points see Jaakko Hintikka, 'Different Kinds of Equivocation in Aristotle,' *Journal of the History of Philosophy*, IX (July, 1971), 369ff., and Hintikka's earlier article, 'Aristotle and the Ambiguity of Ambiguity,' *Inquiry*, II (Autumn, 1959), 137ff.

[67] *Ethica Eudemia* I. 8. 1217^{b}25-35.

form one genus); but if the word is used in virtue of something common, being will fall under one science.⁶⁸

And 'being' for Aristotle meets this requirement:

> There are many senses in which a thing may be said to 'be,' but all that 'is' is related to one central point (πρὸς ἕν), one definite kind of thing, and is not said to 'be' by a mere ambiguity (ὁμωνύμως).⁶⁹

'Healthy' is said to have focal meaning by virtue of having various senses which when expressed in words 'focus on' or refer to one and the same thing, health. For example, when 'healthy' is predicated of a complexion, it means 'indicative of health,' whereas when 'healthy' is predicated of a daily walk, it means 'productive of health.' ⁷⁰ In like manner, 'is' (or 'being') is said to have focal meaning, since its various senses systematically depend on a basic sense, 'being a substance' which refers to one thing, substance. For example, in the sentence 'Socrates is sitting,' 'is' signifies a position of a substance, whereas in the sentence 'Socrates is,' 'is' means 'is a substance.' In fact, 'being' signifies the being of all the kinds of reality specified by the categories— substance, quality of a substance, quantity of a substance, relation, activity, passivity, place, time, position, and state of a substance.⁷¹

It seems that we may formulate the following as a criterion of focal meaning: ⁷²

> a word *w* has focal meaning if: (a) *w* admits of different senses which are not totally distinct; and (b) these various senses (expressible in phrases or λόγοι) are dependent on one basic sense of *w*.

'Being' meets the above conditions, for the basic sense of 'being' is 'being a substance' and the other senses of 'being' are dependent on this sense. (The basic sense is the one that is included in the formulations of all the other senses of the word with focal meaning.)

---

⁶⁸ *Metaphysica K*. 3. 1060ᵇ31-36 (Oxford translation).
⁶⁹ *Metaph*. Γ. 2. 1003ᵃ33-34 (Oxford trans.).
⁷⁰ *Metaph. K*. 3. 1061ᵃ5-7. These senses, but not the examples for 'healthy' are Aristotle's.
⁷¹ *Cat*. 4. 1ᵇ25-2ᵃ10; *Metaph*. Γ. 2. 1003ᵇ5-10; *Metaph*. Δ. 7. 1017ᵃ22-27.
⁷² Strictly speaking, for Aristotle things are homonymous when the same word is predicated of them but in two different senses (*Cat*. 1. 1ᵃ1-2). Focal meaning, in a similar manner, could be said to apply to things of which word *w* is predicated, *w* meeting the conditions laid down above. Aristotle clearly talks about *words* being homonymous in the *Soph. El.*, e.g., 4. 165ᵇ30-35.

Clearly, focal meaning permits Aristotle to shed the view that if a word has various senses, then it is homonymous without qualification, in which case those things of which it is predicated fail to form one genus, and do not fall under one science. Those things of which a word with focal meaning is predicated, on the other hand, may indeed form one genus [73] and fall under one science; e.g., those things of which 'being' is predicated. Hence, Aristotle's special doctrine of focal meaning makes possible the science of being *qua* being. It may be noted that Galen wrote two (now lost) books on πολλαχῶς λεγόμενα [74] but that this notion plays no explicit role in his theory of ambiguity in *De Captionibus*. If challenged presumably Galen would classify focal meaning as a species of homonymy.

---

[73] 'Genus' here is not used strictly, since the categories are the greatest genera, properly speaking.

[74] Galen, *De Libris Propriis* (Kühn ed.) Vol. XIX, p. 45.

CHAPTER FOUR

'LEXIS' AND GALEN'S GENERAL THEORY OF LANGUAGE

Although the title of Galen's treatise suggests a tract strictly on fallacy due to *lexis*, *De Captionibus* is also (and is primarily of interest to us as) a treatise on λέξις itself. I translate *'lexis'* as 'language' except as it occurs in the formulaic name of the Aristotelian fallacy 'εἶδος τῆς λέξεως,' which I translate 'form of expression.'[1] *'Lexis'* does not mean 'style' or 'diction'[2] in *De Captionibus* and it does not correspond to *lexis* in the Stoic sense; namely, articulate sound that does not necessarily convey meaning.[3]

For Galen *lexis* is both spoken and written language; that is, articulate sound and the symbols for articulate sound that convey meaning.[4] Since Galen has this dual conception of language, he would seem to fall in the class of Hockett's laymen:

> The linguist distinguishes between *language* and writing, whereas the layman tends to confuse the two. The layman's terms 'spoken language' and 'written language' suggest that speech and writing are namely two different manifestations of something fundamentally the same. Often enough, the layman thinks that writing is somehow more basic than speech. Almost the reverse is true.[5]

In Galen's defense it may be said that written language is more basic than spoken language in the sense that some fallacies due

---

[1] The rendering 'form of expression' conforms to the Oxford and Loeb translations of Aristotle's fallacy of the same name. The only other Greek word in *De Captionibus* which is rendered 'language' is 'διάλεκτος', which occurs once, at 96,1.

[2] Often in earlier literature, *'lexis'* means diction or style; e.g., Plato *Leges* 795e2, and Aristotle *Ars Poetica* 6. 1449b34.

[3] See Diogenes Laertius *Vitae Philosophorum* 7. 57. For the Stoics, a parrot is capable of *lexis*, but only men are capable of language (*logos*). See *infra* pp. 120-21.

[4] Galen, *De Placitis* 2 (Mueller ed.) Vol. I, p. 195 ll. 3-4, and Galen, *Commentarius III in Hippocratis lib. III Epidemiorum* (Kühn ed.) Vol. XVII, p. 758.

[5] Charles F. Hockett, *A Course in Modern Linguistics* (New York: The Macmillan Company, 1958), p. 4.

to language (e.g., Accent,⁶ Combination and Division) occur predominantly in 'written language.' In any case, it is clear that in *De Captionibus* the focus of the inquiry is as much on written as on spoken language.

Russell's description of pre-Austinian philosophical conceptions of language seems to apply perfectly to Galen:

> Philosophers, being bookish and theoretical folk, have been interested in language chiefly as a means of making statements and conveying information, but this is only one of its purposes . . .⁷

For Galen, not only is signifying the function of language, but it is its essence as well—what does not signify fails to be language (94,16-17). Galen is quite explicit about the use of language in *De Placitis*:

> We use names and linguistic communication (διάλεκτος) generally in order to express the thought in our mind that we have gained from examining the nature of things.⁸

This conception of the use of language seems a legacy of the theory of Plato's *Cratylus*, which holds that a use of language (more precisely, of *names*) is to enable men to teach things to one another,⁹ that is, to convey information.

Galen's general theory of language takes as its basis the notion of language as a vehicle for the transmission of information. This theory consists in a classification of the degrees of clarity of communication that a language may possess. Besides shedding light on Galen's understanding of language, this theory provides a framework for Galen's theory of ambiguity. At any rate, this general theory of language specifies four ways in which language, as a set of words and sentences, signifies: (I) *well*, i.e., lucidly; (II) *badly* (ambiguously), i.e., obscurely with qualification within a linguistic community; (III) *not at all*, i.e., obscurely without qualification within a linguistic community; and (IV) *not at all*

---

⁶ Henceforth, the names of the Aristotelian and Galenic modes of ambiguity, not just their corresponding fallacies, will begin with a capital letter.

⁷ Bertrand Russell, *Human Knowledge: Its Scope and Limits*, Clarion Books (New York: Simon and Schuster, 1948), p. 57. For Russell, expressing emotion and communicating are its primary purposes.

⁸ *De Placitis* 9 (Müller ed.) Vol. I, p. 734, ll. 2-5 (DeLacy translation). 'Thought in our mind' renders 'τὰς κατὰ τὴν ψυχὴν δόξας.'

⁹ *Cratylus* 388a10.

relative to other linguistic communities. I propose to articulate the conditions for language signifying with these degrees of clarity, so as to lend some rigor to Galen's analysis.

I begin with the conditions for a word signifying well:

> a *word* of language L *signifies well* if and only if it means precisely one thing to users [10] of L; i.e., it admits of only one paraphrase, or it admits of more than one paraphrase, all of which are paraphrases of one another.

For example, 'onlooker' in English signifies well, for it means precisely one thing to users of English. It admits of the paraphrases 'a person who watches without taking part' (a statement of the definition of 'onlooker'), and 'spectator' (a synonym of 'onlooker'), both of which are paraphrases of one another.

It may be noted that a word's signifying well is specified in terms of the word's having a uniform sense, expressible in paraphrases that are paraphrases of one another, not in terms of the word's reference (e.g., referring or purporting to refer to only one extra-linguistic entity). Proper names like 'Gerald Ford' and 'Pegasus' are words that have little or no sense, but each refers to or purports to refer to one and only one entity, the 38th President of the United States and the winged horse of Bellerophon. Although Galen does not deal with the special case of the proper name, it seems as though he would want to say that such terms (those that refer only and have no distinguishable sense), in addition to other words which have no sense independent of that which they contribute to the sentence as a whole in which they occur (e.g., articles, certain connectives [11]), do 'signify well' in an attenuated sense—namely, if they occur in sentences that signify well.

The conditions for a sentence signifying well are as follows:

> a *sentence* of language L *signifies well* if and only if it means precisely one thing to users of L; i.e., it admits of one sentential paraphrase, or it admits of more than one such paraphrase, all of which are paraphrases of one another.

The differences between a sentence's and a word's signifying well are most clearly perceived in the sorts of paraphrase[12] which

---

[10] The users of language L include every person who is properly described as knowing L.

[11] An example of such a connective is 'or' (ἤ).

[12] On paraphrases and their relations, see *supra* pp. 12-13.

cases of each admit. Paraphrases of a word that signifies well either express one of its definitions [13] or consist of a synonymous word or phrase. Paraphrases of a sentence that signifies well will be paraphrases consisting of complete sentences, in which (normally) something is predicated of something else, and thus they will be paraphrases in which information is conveyed.

The sentence 'The vacation lasted a fortnight' signifies well, for it means one thing—it admits of the following two paraphrases which are paraphrases of one another: 'The vacation lasted two weeks' and 'It was a two week vacation.' On Galen's theory, the *virtue* of language is identified with signifying well,[14] although he does not use the term 'σαφής' or 'σαφήνεια' (lucidity, clarity) in *De Captionibus*.[15]

The vice of language, on the other hand, is signifying badly, which means signifying ambiguously, and for a word it may be specified as follows:

> a *word* of language *L signifies badly* if and only if it means more than one thing to users of *L*; i.e., it admits of two or more paraphrases that are not paraphrases of one another.

Galen's own example of a word that signifies badly is 'κύων,' since it has several senses—'canine animal,' 'Cynic philosopher,' and 'dogstar'—but not one definite and distinct sense (96,9-10).

In *De Placitis* Galen cites another example of a word that signifies badly, which happens to be the preposition 'ἀπό' ('from').

---

[13] A word, of course, may have two or more definitions.

[14] In *On the Natural Faculties* 1. 1., Galen states that the greatest virtue of language (ἡ μεγίστη λέξεως ἀρετή) is σαφήνεια (clarity, lucidity).

[15] The origins of the doctrine of the virtue of language (or 'style') may be traced to Aristotle. At *Rhet*. 3. 2. 1404ᵇ1-3, the virtue of language, style, or diction (λέξις) is said to be σαφής, and Aristotle states that a sign of this is that if it (λόγος) does not make its meaning plain, it does not perform its function (ἔργον). G. M. A. Grube, in *The Greek and Roman Critics* (Toronto: University of Toronto Press, 1965), p. 95, writes, 'Aristotle will only recognize one virtue (ἀρετή) of style, which is lucidity, since the purpose of speech is to make one's meaning clear. He does indeed recognize other qualities and discusses them at length, but lucidity is the only specific *aretê* or excellence which fulfills the proper function of speech.' Following up Aristotle's *Rhet*., Theophrastus enumerates four virtues of speech, ἑλληνισμός (good Greek), σαφήνεια (clarity), πρέπον (appropriateness), and κατασκευή (elaboration). On Theophrastus' account, see Grube, p. 107. The Stoics also have a doctrine of the virtues of language—good Greek, clarity, conciseness, appropriateness, and elaboration. See Diog. Laert. 7. 59.

It is said to mean both 'ὑπό' ('by agency of') and 'ἐξ' ('out of').¹⁶ Hence, there is reason to believe that Galen's theory extends to other word classes besides common nouns and verbs.

Sentential bad (i.e., ambiguous) signifying may be formulated in this way:

> a *sentence* of language L *signifies badly* if and only if it means more than one thing to users of L; i.e., it admits of at least two sentential paraphrases that are not paraphrases of one another.

Clearly, any ambiguous sentence will be a case of bad signifying. It will signify obscurely ¹⁷ with qualification since it signifies more than one thing rather than signifying one thing distinctly.

A more radical sort of obscurity than that engendered be merely ambiguous language is that which signifies not at all within a linguistic community—language which is obscure without qualification. For a word, it may be specified as follows:

> a *word* of language L *signifies not at all* if and only if it fails to mean even one thing to users of L; it does not admit of paraphrase.

An example of such a word might be '*blituri*'.¹⁸ Neither as a mere articulate sound (phonological unit) nor as an orthographical representation of that sound does it mean anything—it admits of no paraphrase. In fact, Galen does not countenance it as language, for such a 'word' is masquerading as a part of language but is not really a linguistic unit at all. Just as a man who pretends to be a flute-player but who cannot actually play the flute is not a flute-player, so '*blituri*' pretends to be a significant word, but is not,

---

¹⁶ *De Placitis* 2 (Müller ed.) Vol. I, p. 213, ll. 6-13. The premise of Zeno of Citium that contains this ambiguity is at p. 205. ll. 15-16: 'If vocal sound (φωνή) were sent forth from (ἀπό) the brain, then it would not be sent forth through (διά) the pharynx.' (my translation)

¹⁷ Galen may have borrowed this notion of obscurity from Aristotle. It is, after all, the negation of clarity as the virtue of language. At *Top.* 5. 2. 129ᵇ35-130ᵃ4, Aristotle states: '... one must not use as signifying *property* either a word or an expression which is used with several meanings, because anything which has several meanings renders the statement obscure, since he who is about to argue is doubtful which of the various meanings his opponent intends.' (adapted Loeb translation) For more on obscurity in Aristotle see *Rhet*. 3. 3. 1406ᵇ5ff., and 3. 5. 1407ᵇ12ff.

¹⁸ '*Blituri*' is the Stoic example of speech (*lexis*) which is ἄσημος (insignificant), at Diog. Laert. 7. 57. 'ἄσημος' is one of Galen's terms for 'obscure' at 96,7. (His other term is 'ἀσαφής', at 96,7).

and hence is not a constituent of language (94,12-13). Again, proper names, which do not admit of paraphrase, but rather name or purport to name extra-linguistic entities, would seem to qualify as words which signify not at all on this reading of Galen. If confronted with this consequence of his theory, Galen might have produced another definition of a word signifying not at all (which permits proper names to signify well 'in an attenuated sense')[19] as follows:

> a *word* of language L *signifies not at all* (in a loose sense) if and only if it is impossible for that word to occur (be used) in a sentence that either signifies well or signifies badly for users of L.

Clearly, *'blituri'* would be such a word, and 'Roosevelt' and 'or' would not.

The conditions for a sentence not signifying at all may be specified in this way:

> a *sentence* of language L *signifies not at all* if and only if it fails to mean even one thing to users of L; i.e., it does not admit of sentential paraphrase.

An example of such a sentence would be, 'The erpt is on the orpt,' which uses (not mentions) two insignificant words. The fact that the grammatical subject of the sentence is an unintelligible word (in the strict sense) and that the predicate 'is on the orpt' contains such a word prevents the sentence from admitting of paraphrase. A string like Plato's 'runs, walks, sleeps' [20] fails to be a sentence that signifies not at all because it is not a sentence, and because it does not admit of sentential paraphrase, though each of its terms may be individually paraphrased. This string would probably not count as a sentence on Galen's view since it fails to meet minimal syntactic requirements for sentencehood.[21]

Galen rightly claims that no one would accept or propose a

---

[19] See *supra* p. 34.
[20] Plato *Sophista* 262ᵇ5.
[21] At 98,5-7, Galen defines a sentence as a combination of words, and he includes as words, verbs and nouns (names). For Plato, a string fails to be a sentence if it does not meet both syntactic requirements (combining ὀνόματα and ῥήματα, *Soph.* 262c2-5), and semantic requirements (predicating an action of a thing, *Soph.* 262e12-14, and bearing a truth value, *Soph.* 263a11-263b3). Galen does not explicitly introduce these semantic considerations, but they are presupposed by the notion of a sentence conveying information, which seems to be a basic tenet of his doctrine of signification.

premise expressed in language that signifies not at all, i.e., obscurely without qualification (96,6-7). Furthermore, he maintains that such premises (or sentences) are the destruction of language, by which he presumably means that a language constituted solely of such sentences would cease to be language (96,13-14).

The fourth way in which language may signify is *not at all relative* to a speaker of a different language. Clearly language may signify in either of the first three ways (well, badly, not at all) and still signify *not at all relative* to another linguistic community. The conditions for this type of signifying may be specified as follows:

> a *word w* of language *L signifies not at all relative* to users of another language *M* if and only if *w* fails to mean anything to users of *M* who do not know *L*; i.e., *w* fails to admit of paraphrase for them.

> a *sentence s* of language *L signifies not at all relative* to users of another language *M* if and only if *s* fails to mean anything to users of *M* who do not know *L*; i.e., *s* fails to admit of paraphrase for them.

Such a notion is presupposed by Galen's claim that although the foreign languages Persian and Ethiopian do not signify 'for us' (i.e., for those who know Greek to the exclusion of Persian and Ethiopian), we may judge Persian superior to Ethiopian (94,20-96,2). We do so on the basis of their comparative sound, not in respect of how well they signify (96,2-3).[22] (The precise point that Galen is making in this passage is that language that does not signify at all for us may still have accidental virtues, like sonority and calligraphy (94,18-20)).

In sum, we find that Galen's general theory of language is a theory of signification in terms of word and sentence meaning. His general theory clearly indicates the extent to which logical or scientific considerations dominate his inquiry into the nature of language. The degree of clarity with which a sentence signifies is a mark of type of argument of which it may be a constituent. If the premises and conclusion of an argument signify well, then the argument will not be a fallacy due to language, whereas if an inference depends on a premise or conclusion which signifies

---

[22] Galen does not consider the possibility of words and sentences that are common, either phonologically or orthographically, to two languages, but which have different meanings.

badly, then the argument may be a fallacy due to language. Those sentences that signify not at all cannot be part of any argument. It may be noted that this theory, which is designed to describe the nature and function of language, omits all reference to the acts performable through the utterances of sentences[23] besides that of conveying information.[24] In any case, Galen's general theory of language, specifying four ways in which language may function (well, badly, not at all, not at all relatively), provides a framework within which one may more sharply focus on the notion of ambiguity, which is what signifying badly amounts to.

---

[23] J. L. Austin claims that the utterance of certain sentences constitutes speech acts, so-called 'illocutionary acts,' like promising, apologizing, thanking, sympathizing, cursing, etc., and holds that there are more than 1000 such acts. See his *How To Do Things with Words*, ed. by J. O. Urmson, Galaxy Books (New York: Oxford University Press, 1965), pp. 149, 159.

[24] For Galen of course, conveying information is not a speech act. It is an attribute of sentences that signify well or badly.

CHAPTER FIVE

GALEN'S THEORY OF AMBIGUITY

The main original contribution of Galen's *De Captionibus* to the philosophy of language in antiquity is a theoretical description of linguistic ambiguity. Galen's achievement may be described as an exhaustive classification (including definitions by genus and differentia) of every sort of ambiguity that occurs in language.[1] Galen's theory is designed both to yield a deeper insight into linguistic ambiguity and to reveal the true nature of this phenomenon.

Briefly, in his theory Galen appeals to five principles which govern all cases of ambiguity in language: *Actuality, Potentiality, Appearance, Being Lexical,* and *Being Syntactic*. Galen proceeds by accepting as 'givens' both Aristotle's enumeration of the types of ambiguity [2] and the following preliminary definition of sentential ambiguity:

> an ambiguous sentence =df. a sentence, the utterance or inscription of which has at least two distinct meanings.[3]

From there he classifies and defines the types of ambiguity he himself countenances as follows:

> Homonymy =df. actual, lexical ambiguity
> Amphiboly =df. actual, syntactic ambiguity
> Accent =df. potential, lexical ambiguity
> Combination and Division =df. potential, syntactic ambiguity
> Form of expression$_{(L)}$ =df. apparent, lexical ambiguity
> Form of expression$_{(S)}$ =df. apparent, syntactic ambiguity

Galen claims that his method [4] shows that any case of ambiguity

---

[1] It is intended to apply to ancient Greek, but may be modified to apply to other natural languages, like English. See *infra* p. 45, n. 19.

[2] We recall that Galen misreads Aristotle on this topic since three of the latter's modes (Accent, Combination, Division) are cases of linguistic confusion, not of ambiguity. See *supra* pp. 24-28.

[3] As reformulated here, Galen lifts this from *Soph. El.* 4. 165^{b}29-30. See 90,20-21.

[4] See *infra* pp. 50-52, and 104,3-5.

in language will fall under one of these jointly exhaustive and mutually exclusive headings.[5]

Now that Galen's theory has been expounded in skeletal form, I turn to describing more completely the substance of the theoretical principles he invokes. Only a detailed analysis of the scope, content, and implications of Galen's theory will do justice to his insight into this linguistic and logical problem. His theory is constructed to characterize and explain ambiguity as it occurs in *sentences*.[6] This focus on sentential ambiguity reflects Galen's intent in *De Captionibus* to discuss the role of ambiguity in producing fallacious arguments—and such ambiguity will be sentential (i.e., it will concern either the premise or the conclusion of such an argument).

According to Galen's theory, for any ambiguous sentence, its ambiguity will be either lexical or syntactic, and actual, potential, or apparent. The notion of lexical ambiguity is relatively unproblematic. A sentence is *lexically ambiguous* when one of its words has more than one sense, even when that word is isolated from the sentence in question. For example, 'The object is light' is a case of lexical ambiguity because the adjective 'light' has two senses ('of little weight,' 'pale in color'), and it accounts for the sentence being ambiguous.

The notion of syntactic ambiguity is a bit more complicated, and here one struggles to resist the temptation to discern contemporary linguistic insight in the meager account Galen provides for it. A sentence is said to be *syntactically ambiguous* not when one of its words has more than one sense, but rather when its ambiguity derives from the sentence as such, (αὐτὸς ὁ λόγος, 88,10); that is, from the *combination* of its words. Presumably Galen means by 'αὐτὸς ὁ λόγος,' the structure of the sentence which is syntactically ambiguous, and his brief analyses of syntactic ambiguity at 88,11-13 and 90,1-2 support this interpretation.

According to traditional grammar, a sentence that is syntactically ambiguous is one that admits of more than one parsing. This disposition of the sentence reveals the ambiguity of its structure that in turn causes the sentence to be ambiguous. Galen seems

---

[5] That Galen's modes are intended to be mutually exclusive is indirectly shown by his criticism of the Stoic enumeration of the kinds of ambiguity. Galen attacks their teaching on the grounds that the kinds of ambiguity they list are not mutually exclusive (108,9-10). See *infra* p. 82, n. 31.

[6] See 98,3-5.

to identify what may be termed 'deep' and 'superficial' species of syntactic ambiguity. An example of 'deep' syntactic ambiguity is Galen's illustration of Amphiboly: γένοιτο καταλαβεῖν τὸν ὗν ἐμέ [7] (88,11). Such ambiguity is 'deep' (or Actual, for Galen) in that punctuation or pause alone cannot resolve it. The ambiguity results from the fact that two words in the sentence ('ὗν' and 'ἐμέ') can both assume more than one grammatical role; in this case, either word may be subject or object of the infinitive. About this sentence, Galen says only that its ambiguity is due to the sentence as such, which may be taken in an active or passive sense (i.e., to catch or to be caught by the boar, 88,12-13).

'Superficial' syntactic ambiguity (or Potential, for Galen) is illustrated by Galen's example of Combination and Division: Πεντήκοντ' ἀνδρῶν ἑκατὸν λίπε δῖος Ἀχιλλεύς [8] (88,18). Galen explains that the difference in meaning of the sentence 'depends upon whether 'men' is considered combined with or separated from 'fifty',' (90,1-2). Now, although this ambiguity may be analyzed as a case of 'deep' syntactic ambiguity, in which both 'ἑκατόν' and 'πεντήκοντα' may play more than one syntactic role (each may be either object of 'λίπε' or partitive genitive with 'ἀνδρῶν'), it seems that Galen is here identifying a less serious form of ambiguity, what has been called *ambiguity of grouping*.[9] Such ambiguity is syntactic in that it involves a question of what is to be construed with what, but it is 'superficial' in that it is mechanically resoluble in a way that does not alter the words in the sentence. Such a sentence is easily disambiguated by pause or punctuation. Such ambiguity is a matter of detail, the minor question of what modifies what that is simply resolved, rather than a question of 'deep' syntactic ambiguity which no amount of punctuation or pausing could cure.[10]

These remarks on syntactic ambiguity anticipate some of the interpretation of *actual* and *potential* ambiguity which follows.

---

[7] Translation: 'May it happen that I catch the wild boar' and 'May it happen that the wild boar catch me.'

[8] Translation: 'Noble Achilles left a hundred of fifty men' and 'Noble Achilles left fifty of a hundred men.'

[9] Quine (*Word and Object*), p. 137. Quine's example of ambiguity of grouping is the phrase 'pretty little girls' camp.'

[10] It may be noted that there is another possible rendering for the sentence in question; namely, 'Noble Achilles left 150 of the men.' But this reading is not specifiable, as opposed to the others, by adding certain punctuation and pauses. See *infra* pp. 117-18.

What is *actually* ambiguous for Galen is that which in fact means two things as uttered or inscribed (98,15-16). An example of Amphiboly (actual, syntactic ambiguity) has been discussed above,[11] as has a case of Homonymy (actual, lexical ambiguity).[12] The point about an *actually* ambiguous sentence is that, as it stands, it *has* two meanings. A *potentially* ambiguous sentence, on the contrary, as it stands *can* have two meanings corresponding to the two (or more) orthographical and phonological changes that it can undergo (which however, fail to produce another sentence). This seems to be what Galen means when he states that a potentially ambiguous sentence is one that means exactly one thing, but *can* mean more than one thing.

An example will clarify Galen's meaning. Consider his example of Combination and Division which we have already briefly discussed, but written without any diacritical marks or pronounced without pause between any of the words:

(s) Πεντήκοντ' ἀνδρῶν ἑκατὸν λίπε δῖος Ἀχιλλεύς.

For Galen, (s), as it stands, is potentially ambiguous, for (s) can signify either of two things, both of which are specified by the sentence (s) when diacritical marks [13] have been added or when pronounced with pause between some of the words. Presumably there are two other ways to inscribe and utter (s), which are:

(s_1) Πεντήκοντ' ἀνδρῶν, ἑκατὸν λίπε δῖος Ἀχιλλεύς
(s_2) Πεντήκοντ', ἀνδρῶν ἑκατὸν λίπε δῖος Ἀχιλλεύς

(When uttered, the comma indicates the placement of pause.) (s_1) means exactly one thing; to wit, 'Noble Achilles left a hundred of fifty men.' And (s_2) means exactly one thing: namely, 'Noble Achilles left fifty of a hundred men.'

---

[11] See *supra* p. 42.
[12] See *supra* p. 41. Galen's example of Homonymy is at 88,9, 'κύνα τεθήρακα.'
[13] Jannaris, (in *Historical Greek Grammar*, p. 67), states that 'The form of our modern comma (,) was also known [among the Alexandrian grammarians] and called ὑποδιαστολή or (βραχεῖα) διαστολή, but served in the 'scriptura continua' to separate two words liable to confusion, as: ΕΣΤΙΝ,ΟΥΣ and ΕΣΤΙ,ΝΟΥΣ. It is still sometimes used as a distinctive mark, as ὅ, τι = 'whatever,' ὅτι = 'that'.' Presumably the ὑποδιαστολή also functioned to indicate which terms were to be construed with which other terms. Dionysius Thrax's term for comma is 'ὑποστιγμή' in *Ars Grammatica*, in *Grammatici Graeci* I, 1. ed. by G. Uhlig (Leipzig: Teubner, 1883), p. 7, l. 6.

Galen's description of potential ambiguity seems to presuppose the following criterion of sentential identity: two sentences are the same if they have the same combination of words. This should not come as a surprise. After all, for Galen a sentence is a combination of *words* (98,5-6), notwithstanding the occurrence of pause or any diacritical mark.[14] Hence, though three entities are specified in the analysis of the above case of potential ambiguity, (s), (s_1), and (s_2), on Galen's theory they are the same sentence, (s) is potentially ambiguous in that it *can* mean either of two things (i.e., what is expressed by (s_1) and (s_2)), and (s) qua (s_1) means exactly one thing, as does (s) qua (s_2).

Accent, the potential *lexical* mode of ambiguity, may be explained along similar lines. For example,

(t) ορος εστηκεν

inscribed without accentual marks (including breathings) or perhaps uttered with indistinct or blurred pitch accent and breathings, can mean either of two things, which are specified by

(t_1) ὅρος ἕστηκεν
(t_2) ὅρος ἕστηκεν

each [15] of which is identical with (t), but has breathings and accents added. Accentuation (and breathings) are not constituent parts of a sentence, or for that matter of a word according to Galen.[16] Hence, Galen's theory assumes not only the criterion of sentential identity formulated above, but also the following criterion of lexical identity: two words are the same if they have the same letters in the same sequence.[17] And in this way, 'ὅρος,' 'ὅρος,' and 'ορος' all count as one word on Galen's account. If they were different words, Galen might argue, then of course there would be no ambiguity involved, and such a line of reasoning is the one that Aristotle seems to have adopted (although Galen fails to appreciate this). Aristotle

---

[14] See 110,15-16.
[15] (t_1) may be rendered 'a hill stands,' and (t_2) as 'a boundary stands.' I put aside the complication that 'ὅρος' itself is a homonym, meaning 'definition,' and 'term' in addition to 'boundary.'
[16] See 110,15-16.
[17] If we ignore the part about an additional sign, it appears that Galen agrees with the criterion of lexical identity proposed by Aristotle at *Soph. El.* 20. 177b4-6, which is quoted *supra* p. 28.

concludes that Accent is not a case of ambiguity, but instead of linguistic confusion.[18]

At first glance the proposed analysis of Galen's notion of potential lexical ambiguity seems to conflict with a remark of our philosopher at 100,8-9. There Galen states that in applying accents, *one word* is transformed into *another*. But on the analysis offered above, 'ὅρος' and 'ὄρος' are the same word for Galen. Such apparent contradiction may be resolved by reference to Galen's intention at 100,8-9. For in that passage Galen is attempting to point out how the division of a compound word (presumably by pause or addition of a diacritical sign) produces a phrase rather than another word, (the result of adding accents). For purposes of explanation Galen seems here to have reverted to ordinary parlance, according to which 'ὅρος' and 'ὄρος' are distinct words. If this remark appears to conflict with our analysis, it is only because Galen is not speaking guardedly at 100,8-9, and he need not do so for the purpose at hand.[19]

In contrast to his discussion of actual and potential ambiguity, Galen devotes scant space to the principle of Appearance. He tells us that for any object, it exists potentially, actually, or apparently (in appearance). If something exists *apparently*, then presumably it only *appears* to be what it is, but in fact *is* something else. In any case, this is Aristotle's sense of being apparent.[20] Hence, a sentence which is apparently ambiguous only appears to have two meanings. In fact, it signifies one thing, but because of the language in which it is expressed, it appears to (but really does not) signify something else (90,2-3).

At 102,13-14 Galen specifies that apparent ambiguity is both

---

[18] See *supra* pp. 26-28.
[19] I. M. Copi, in *Introduction to Logic* (4th ed.; New York: The Macmillan Co., 1972), pp. 94-95, has suggested an English parallel for ambiguity of accent in Greek, in terms of word stress (in speech) and italicization (in written language). His example is 'We should not speak ill of our friends.' If it remains unaccented, it may be paraphrased 'We should not malign our friends,' but if 'friends' is accented, the sentence may be paraphrased, 'Only our friends should we not malign.' Clearly these two paraphrases are not paraphrases of one another, so the original sentence is ambiguous, and is so because of accent.
[20] See *Soph. El.* 1. 164ᵇ23-165ᵃ24. There Aristotle remarks that tin *appears* to be silver, but is not silver, and that the sophistic art is said to consist in *apparent* and not real wisdom.

lexical and syntactic, and refers his readers elsewhere for examples.²¹ But earlier Galen provided an example of lexical ambiguity; to wit, 'ἀκούω' ('I hear'), which is apparently ambiguous in that it appears to signify an activity (since it is an active Greek verb), but in fact signifies a passivity, the logical category to which hearing properly belongs.²² The mode that is classified under the heading of and defined as apparent lexical ambiguity, I term 'Form of expression (L).'

An example of apparent syntactic ambiguity, 'Form of expression (S)' may be found in Galen's *Institutio Logica*. There Galen claims that the sentence 'If it is not day, then it is night,' expressed (as it is) in the conditional form of speech (ἐν σχήματι λέξεως συνημμένῳ), is called a conditional by those who pay attention to the sound (φωνή), but an exclusive disjunction (διεζευγμένον) by those who pay heed to what is really meant.²³ That is, it appears to be a conditional because of the form in which it is expressed, but it is really an exclusive disjunction. The distinct meanings of a conditional and an exclusive disjunction are reflected in their respective truth conditions. In the former case the sentence is false if and only if the antecedent is true and the consequent false, whereas in the latter case, the sentence is false if and only if the antecedent and consequent have the same truth value, (be it truth or falsity).

One might ask what kind of syntactic ambiguity affects the above example, and the answer seems to lie in what Quine has called 'ambiguity of certain constructions.'²⁴ That is, the ambiguity is not due to 'syntactical ambiguity in a fuller sense: ambiguities of structure, ambiguity as to what is syntactically connected with what,' ²⁵ but rather to the ambiguity of the 'εἰ μή'

---

²¹ Elsewhere includes Eudemus' Περὶ Λέξεως and, I suggest, Galen's *Institutio Logica*.

²² See *infra* p. 71.

²³ In Greek the example is 'εἰ μὴ ἡμέρα ἐστί, νύξ ἐστιν,' in Galen's *Institutio Logica* 3. 5. (Kalbfleisch ed.), p. 9, ll. 9-16. This passage has been translated by Benson Mates (in *Stoic Logic*, pp. 117-118), as follows: ' "If it is not day, then it is night," ... when it is said in a conditional form of speech, is called a 'conditional' by those who pay attention to the sounds only, but a 'disjunction' by those who pay attention to the nature of what is meant. Similarly, such a form of speech as "If it is not night, then it is day" is a disjunctive proposition by the nature of what is meant, but in speech it has the form of a conditional.'

²⁴ Quine (*Word and Object*), p. 135.

²⁵ *Ibid.* For further analysis of such ambiguity, see *infra* pp. 65-66.

('if not,' 'unless') construction, when the antecedent and consequent are contradictories.[26]

Having examined the theoretical principles with which Galen has erected his theory of ambiguity, we may appreciate his success in articulating a coherent and fairly sophisticated account of this linguistic phenomenon. Galen's major advance on Aristotle is his exhaustive classification of the species of ambiguity (three of which, strictly speaking, Aristotle does not recognize as ambiguity). Crude as Galen's account may appear from the viewpoint of present day transformational linguistics, it is plain that the sentences Galen analyzes are of the same sort that contemporary linguists consider. Galen's introduction of the notion of 'potential' (or 'superficial') ambiguity to describe certain forms of syntactic ambiguity and his method of resolving such ambiguity clearly seem to anticipate the analyses (and recommendations for disambiguation) made by contemporary philosophers of language [27] for similar sentences.[28] Furthermore, Galen's stubborn refusal to subsume apparent ambiguity under any other species qualifies him (along with Aristotle and Plato [29]) as a forerunner of what has been called the fundamental insight of twentieth century analytic philosophy, which focuses on a logical critique of language; namely, 'that grammatical similarity might conceal logical dissimilarity.'[30]

There is little doubt that Galen's systematic theory affords a deeper understanding of the notion of ambiguity than existed

---

[26] Another example of such apparent ambiguity might be the sentence, 'If you are hungry, there are sandwiches on the table' which appears to be an ordinary conditional, but in fact may be analyzed as follows: 'There are sandwiches on the table, and if you are hungry, then you can eat some of them.' Although the surface structure of the sentence is that of a simple conditional introduced by 'if,' the sentence in fact has a more complex logical structure.

[27] For example, W. V. O. Quine, in *Elementary Logic* (rev. ed.; Cambridge, Mass.: Harvard University Press, 1965), pp. 26-27, and Quine (*Word and Object*), p. 137.

[28] It must be granted that Galen was not the first to notice that word grouping and punctuation in language make a difference in what is meant; for example, Aristotle at *Rhet.* 3. 5. 1407^{b}11-25, in his discussion of obscurity in Heraclitus. But for Aristotle, punctuation or word break does not resolve ambiguity in one sentence (as it does for Galen), but rather distinguishes one sentence from another.

[29] See *Statesman* 262D.

[30] Anthony Flew, 'Introduction,' in *Logic and Language*, ed. by Anthony Flew, 1st and 2nd Series, Anchor Books (Garden City: Doubleday & Co., 1965), p. 12.

previously, and it is a tribute to his originality and ability to formulate his intuitions and observations concerning language that contemporary linguists, philosophers of language, and logicians are (unbeknownst to themselves [31]) rediscovering Galenic insight into the problem of ambiguity.

---

[31] An example is Quine, who gives no footnote to Galen in his discussion of ambiguity of grouping (*Word and Object*, p. 137).

CHAPTER SIX

THE SOURCES AND METHOD OF GALEN'S THEORY

Galen's stated purpose in Chapter 3 of *De Captionibus* is to show that the fallacies due to language are six in number. To accomplish this goal, Galen applies a particular method, and, in the process, generates a theoretical account of ambiguity. Here our interest is to discern the nature of the method Galen introduces, its application to the concept of ambiguity, its probable historical sources, and the sources of Galen's theory in general.

In crude terms Galen's method may be characterized as an exercise in conceptual analysis. In more historically accurate terms, however, Galen may be said to be engaging in dialectic of the 'late' Platonic variety—the species of dialectic adumbrated by Socrates in the *Phaedrus* and which is employed in other late dialogues.[1] That Galen was familiar with this method is clear from *De Placitis* 9, where Galen gives his cachet to the 'so called method of division,'[2] and even quotes verbatim the relevant passage in the *Phaedrus* at 265c8-265e3 as follows:

> [Socrates.] My view is that, while it is really hardly more than a pleasant game, still by reason of the fortuitous presence in it of two ways of approaching some of the things it expresses, it is not without value—I mean, if one could acquire with conscious art the power of these two modes of treatment.

---

[1] Late dialogues include (minimally) the *Sophist, Statesman,* and *Philebus.* For a probable chronological ordering of Plato's dialogues (with references) see R. Robinson and J. D. Denniston's 'Plato,' in *Plato: Metaphysics and Epistemology,* ed. by Gregory Vlastos, Anchor Books (Garden City: Doubleday and Co., 1971), p. 15.

[2] See Phillip DeLacy. 'Plato and the Method of the Arts,' in *The Classical Tradition: Literary and Historical Studies in Honor of Harry Caplan,* ed. by Luitpold Wallach (Ithaca: Cornell University Press, 1966), p. 123, and *De Placitis* 9 (Müller ed.) Vol. I, p. 766, ll. 10-15. It is unclear how Galen's use of the method of division in *De Captionibus* is to be reconciled with any one of the four starting points for inquiry recognized in *De Placitis* 2 (Müller ed.) Vol. I, pp. 169ff., i.e., the scientific, dialectic (proceeding from irrelevant premises), rhetorical (proceeding from opinion), and the sophistical (proceeding from ambiguous language). On this classification, see Phillip DeLacy, 'Galen and the Greek Poets,' *Greek, Roman, and Byzantine Studies* VII (1966), 263-65. This unclarity supports Gilbert's view that 'Galen adopted several methodological traditions—and never quite made his own view consistent.' (Gilbert, p. 23.)

> [Phaedrus.] What are they?
> [Soc.] The power to organize into a single comprehensive system the unarranged characteristics of a subject. In this way each subject one may at any time wish to discuss will be perfectly clear through its having been defined. Take, for example, our present discussion of love: the definition of its nature—it doesn't matter for my point whether it is correct or not—has enabled my speech to be clear and self-consistent.
> [Phaedr.] And what do you mean by the other sort of ability, Socrates?
> [Soc.] It is the reverse of the other: the ability to divide into species according to natural articulations, avoiding the attempt to shatter the unity of a natural part, as a clumsy butcher might do.[3]

In Chapter 3 of *De Captionibus* Galen is dividing in the way described above, having collected the six unarranged Aristotelian modes under the unity 'ambiguity' in Chapter 1. It is sentential ambiguity that Galen here subjects to the process of division. His division is not the physical chopping of a whole into parts, but rather metaphorical division (κατὰ μεταφοράν), in which a whole is cut into genera (γένη) and differentia (διαφοραί) or species (εἴδη).[4] Now that the general method Galen employs has been specified, I turn to delineating the precise structure of Galen's division of ambiguity.

There seem to be two bases for this division, or *fundamenta divisionis*—I term them the 'quantitative' and 'qualitative' bases. On the *quantitative* basis, sentential ambiguity is divided as being either lexical or syntactic.[5] And this division which is said to be exhaustive (98,7-9) cuts sentential ambiguity into two mutually exclusive classes.[6] On the *qualitative* basis, ambiguity is exhaustively divided into three mutually exclusive classes, the actual, potential, and apparent. In this way any occurrence of ambiguity will fall under one of the two quantitative headings and under one of the three qualitative headings.

Since Galen's division seems to have more than one basis of

---

[3] *De Placitis* 9 (Müller ed.) Vol. I, pp. 767-68. The translation of this text as it occurs in the *Phaedrus* is by W. C. Helmbold and W. G. Rabinowitz.
[4] *De Placitis* 9 (Müller ed.) Vol. I, p. 826, ll. 1-3.
[5] See *supra* pp. 41-42.
[6] See *supra* pp. 40-41.

division, it would appear to violate one of the canonical rules to be observed in logical division; namely, that 'division must proceed at every stage, and so far as possible through all its stages, upon one principle, or *fundamentum divisionis*.[7] But the qualification, 'so far as possible' (in the quoted rule) admits of division in which the *fundamentum divisionis* is a combination of principles.[8] In the Galenic division of ambiguity, the *fundamentum divisionis* would appear to be the combination of quantitative and qualitative principles.

Joseph provides a model of division in which the *fundamentum divisionis* is a combination (to which Galen's division conforms in the relevant respects) by citing Aristotle's division of 'element,'[9] which is schematized (by Joseph) as follows:

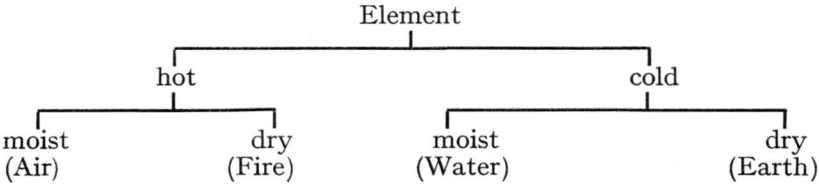

At the first stage of the above division, the principle of division is temperature, whereas at the second it is humidity. Their combination constitutes the *fundamentum divisionis* of the entire division.[10]

Galen's division at 98,7-13 may be schematized as follows:[11]

---

[7] Joseph, p. 104. The other rules are 'A division must be exhaustive,' and 'The constituent species of the genus must exclude each other,' according to Joseph, p. 103.

[8] Joseph, p. 106.

[9] Aristotle *De Generatione et Corruptione* 2. 3. 330ª30-330ᵇ8, cited by Joseph, p. 111.

[10] As Joseph states (pp. 105-106), 'Matter is either hot or cold; matter is either moist or dry; and hence four species were established, the hot and dry, the hot and moist, the cold and dry, the cold and moist. But there is not really a cross-division here. We do not, while professing to divide upon the basis of temperature, at the same time introduce species founded upon the basis of humidity (as if we were to distinguish the hot, cold, and moist elements); our real basis is neither humidity nor temperature, but the combination of the modes of temperature with the modes of humidity. And such a basis offers a peculiarly favourable opportunity for a good division.'

[11] A discussion of the modes that fall under the headings of this division may be found *supra* pp. 40-47, and *infra* pp. 76-79.

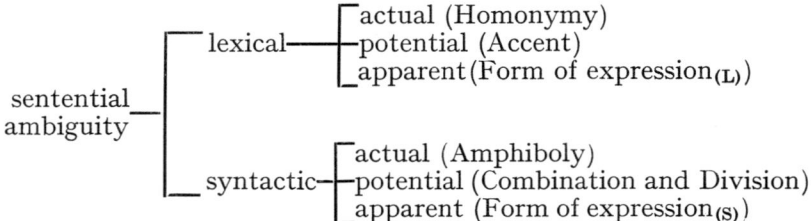

That the quantitative cut is performed at the first stage, and the qualitative at the second, is arbitrary and reflects the order in which Galen makes his division known (98,7-11). This order might be reversed of course, with no ill effects on the result.

One might hold that the above division is inadequate because it is 'non-dichotomous,' arguing that only 'dichotomy'—division that cuts 'the genus at every stage into two members ... which do and do not possess the same differentia' [12]—is useful division. Plato's definition of a statesman in the *Statesman* (e.g., at 258C) generally proceeds by means of dichotomy. Dichotomy is appropriate in that context, however, for the end sought is the definition of one subspecies. But, as Joseph points out, in a division (like Galen's) performed for the purpose of 'classifying or arranging all that is contained in the genus, dichotomy should never be used.' [13] Were it used in the case of ambiguity, at the first cut we should have lexical and non-lexical, and at the second, actual and non-actual members. Clearly this procedure would do Galen no good with regard to his intention of displaying all the parts (species and subspecies) of the concept of ambiguity. It may be granted that Galen wishes to produce definitions for the modes of sentential ambiguity he recognizes, but his non-dichotomous division suffices for this task also.[14]

---

[12] Joseph, p. 107.

[13] *Ibid.* A genus that naturally divides into two species is not necessarily a case of dichotomy. To divide number into odd and even is not the same as dividing it into odd and not odd. On this see Joseph, p. 110. A famous example of dichotomy is in *Isagoge* 3, where Porphyry (who was born thirty-three years after Galen's death) defines 'man'.

[14] It may be noted that non-dichotomous divisions are not rarities in antiquity. For example, Plato divides goods into mental, bodily, and external goods, and mental goods into justice, prudence, courage, temperance, and the like, according to Aristotle's lost work *Diairesis* (in Aristotle *Fragmenta Selecta*, ed. by W. D. Ross (OCT), pp. 101-102, which is also Diog. Laert. 3. 80). The Stoics term dichotomous division 'διαίρεσις,' and call general division (like Galen's) 'μερισμός,' at Diog. Laert. 7. 61.

The word 'μέθοδος' makes its sole occurrence in *De Captionibus* at 104,8, where Galen is saying that Aristotle's account of fallacy due to language is methodically written; that is, that Aristotle's account of the modes of ambiguity conforms to the methodical principles Galen has expounded. 'μέθοδος' would seem to designate both the specific process of division that Galen applies to the concept of ambiguity, and also the art of dialectic (i.e., Collection and Division) that governs this particular division of ambiguity. Presumably it is the art of dialectic (referred to as ἡ τέχνη) which is being compared to the art of medicine later in the treatise at 104,16-18. Gilbert seems to speak directly to this point in the following passage:

> [There is a] peculiar interplay which develops later [than Plato] in Greek thought between *method* in the singular (which refers to Art, and especially to the peculiar Greek art of dialectic) and *methods* in the plural (which are the dialectical devices so beloved of Socrates). The methods can be applied to the 'material' or subject matter of any art, and when so prosecuted result in a particular art, or method.... Only in dialectic do *method* and *methods* merge and become confused. In the other arts the method is the result of the *methods* of dialectic. It goes without saying that the methods or techniques of shoemaking, e.g., as used in our modern sense (say, of how to sew leather or fasten heels), had no interest whatsoever for Socrates, or for the Greek philosophers in general.[15]

It is being suggested here only that Galen's use of 'μέθοδος' at 104,8 illustrates the dual notion of method in antiquity as articulated by Gilbert.

Now that we have examined Galen's method in Chapter 3, we may turn to the historical origins of his two stage division. The division of ambiguity into lexical and syntactic seems to be present in Aristotle's dictum that ambiguity is found in both words and sentences,[16] and Galen explicitly ascribes this distinction to Aristotle.[17] But the origin of the division of ambiguity into actual, potential, and apparent, is less clear. Galen claims that this division is recognizable in Aristotle's ordering when he discusses the modes of ambiguity (104,10-14), but this is not

---

[15] Gilbert, p. 6.
[16] *Soph. El.* 4. 165^{b}29-30.
[17] See 104,8-10.

to say that Aristotle is the one who has proved that 'actually, potentially, and apparently' are the 'only ways of existing or of being spoken of' (98,10-12). We are left with the fact that Galen does not specify the places where it is proved that these three exhaust the ways in which something may exist.

However, because Galen does refer to the works of Eudemus of Rhodes [18] at 102,16 as a source of examples of apparent ambiguity, and because Galen wrote a three book commentary on Eudemus' Περὶ Λέξεως,[19] there seems to be some reason to suspect that the source of the threefold division is Eudemus' book or Galen's commentary on it, or both. Upon turning to the fragments of Eudemus' book [20] (Περὶ Λέξεως), we find that there are only forty-five lines of Greek prose extant, seventeen of which are taken directly from Galen's *De Captionibus*. The four fragments that are not based on Galenic testimony contain no hint of the division in question. Hence, we have no external corroborating evidence, one way or the other.

In his commentary on Eudemus, Wehrli tells us that the subordination of the modes of ambiguity under these three headings *may* indeed be Eudemus' innovation—but Wehrli's evidence is admittedly weak.[21] He bases his tentative position on the fact that systematization in general characterizes Eudemus' handling of Aristotelian doctrine, that ἐνέργεια and δύναμις are Peripatetic concepts, and that φαντασία is a term used by Aristotle at *Sophistici Elenchi* 4. 165ᵇ25 (and elsewhere in that treatise).[22]

Prantl's evidence is a bit more persuasive.[23] He justifies the attribution of the threefold division to Eudemus by reference to Galen's manner of proceeding in Chapter 3 of *De Captionibus*.

---

[18] Aulus Gellius (*Noctes Atticae* 13. 5) reports that Eudemus of Rhodes and Theophrastus excelled the rest of Aristotle's disciples in talent and learning, but that the latter was appointed Aristotle's successor.

[19] Galen, *De Libris Propriis* (Kühn ed.) Vol. XIX, p. 47.

[20] Fritz Wehrli, *Eudemos von Rhodos: Die Schule des Aristoteles*, Texte und Kommentar (Basel: Benno Schwabe & Co., 1955) pp. 20-21.

[21] Wehrli states (p. 86) that 'Die Berufung auf andere Gewährsmänner neben E. verbietet nicht, auch das Einzelne auf diesen zu beziehen, weil Systematisierung im allgemeinen seine Behandlung aristotelischer Lehre kennzeichnet und ἐνέργεια und δύναμις ausserdem peripatetische Begriffe sind; φαντασία ist sogar aus dem oben ausgeschriebenen Text [*Soph. El.*] übernommen.'

[22] Wehrli, p. 86.

[23] Prantl (*Geschichte der Logik*, Vol. I), pp. 398-99.

In Prantl's view,[24] Galen's avoidance of a detailed discussion of apparent ambiguity (while at the same time devoting much space to the other members of the division), and his citation of the works of Eudemus for examples, strongly suggest that the division is that of Eudemus. More properly, however, such reference suggests that Eudemus has explored the area of apparent ambiguity. At any rate, the evidence weakly tends to support the view that the threefold division is the innovation of Eudemus. But no matter. Even if it is original with Eudemus, the complete analysis or division of ambiguity in *De Captionibus*, encompassing both the twofold and the threefold divisions, is Galen's own creation.

---

[24] Prantl writes, (p. 398, n. 92), 'Ich glaube, dass wer die Schreibweise des Galenus kennt, es mir nicht als einen voreiligen Schluss vorwerfen werde, wenn ich die Zurückführung dieser eigenthümlichen Eintheilung auf Eudemus als ihren Urheber aus dem Umstande folgere, dass Galenus . . . indem er den Grund angeben will, warum Aristoteles obige sechs Arten aufzähle, zunächst jene Eintheilung vorführt, und dann, nachdem er bei den zweiten Gliede derselben ziemlich weitschweifig geworden war, für das dritte Glied sich die Mühe weiterer Beispiele spart, dabei aber unmittelbar anknüpfend sagt, die Beispiele könne man aus Eudemus und Anderen nehmen.'

CHAPTER SEVEN

THE STOICS ON FALLACY AND AMBIGUITY

We have scant information about the Stoic teaching on fallacy and ambiguity, although Chrysippus is reputed to have written twenty-one treatises (in forty-eight books) on sophisms and related puzzling arguments,[1] and seven treatises (in seventeen books) on ambiguity.[2] The fragmentary state of the doxographical tradition, including Chapter 4 of *De Captionibus*, does not permit a complete reconstruction of the Stoic theory of fallacy and ambiguity, but it does provide a basis for its partial description. The evidence suggests that at least some of the Stoic interest in ambiguity is generated by their desire to resolve logical and linguistic problems raised by the sophisms they discuss. In what follows an attempt will be made to sketch briefly the Stoic teaching on fallacy, and to systematize (as much as possible) the Stoic doctrine of ambiguity in language.

Certain of the sophisms that concerned the Stoics are said to be the invention of Eubulides, a member of the Megarian [3] School in the fourth century B.C., whereas others seem to have been first proposed by Chrysippus himself (in the third century B.C.). Seven sophisms belong to the first group, which Kneale and Kneale reduce to four types:[4] the *Liar* [5] shows 'the oddity of trying to

---

[1] 'Puzzling argument' is my translation of 'ἄποροι λόγοι.' See *Stoicorum Veterum Fragmenta* (hereafter SVF), ed. by J. von Arnim (Stuttgart: Teubner, 1964), Vol. II, #15-16 (Also, Diog. Laert. 7. 195-198).

[2] SVF II, #14 (Also Diog. Laert. 7. 193). 'ἀμφιβολία' (amphiboly) is the Stoics' general term for ambiguity.

[3] The Megarian School was founded by Euclides, an older contemporary of Plato. Little is known about the school, except that in general it adopted Eleatic doctrine and focused its attention on Zenonian dialectic. Members of the school include Eubulides (to whom Diog. Laert. attributes the Liar antimony, the Disguised, the Electra, the Veiled Figure, the Sorites, the Horned One, and the Bald Head (at 2. 108)); Apollonius Cronus; Diodorus Cronus, (fl. c. 300 B.C., who is credited with the discovery of the Veiled Figure and the Horned One (Diog. Laert. 2. 111)); and Stilpo (380-300 B.C., the teacher of Zeno of Citium (335-263 B.C.), the founder of Stoicism). It may be noted that the Liar and the Horned One are also ascribed to Chrysippus (Diog. Laert. 7. 187).

[4] Kneale and Kneale, p. 114.

[5] According to Mates, (*Stoic Logic*, p. 84), no competent logician of antiquity is known to have solved the Liar antimony. It is proposed in several

make a statement say something about its own truth or falsity;'[6] the *Hooded Man*, the *Unnoticed Man*, or the *Electra*[7] would seem to fall under the Aristotelian heading Accident, although it raises questions about referential opacity and transparency;[8] the *Bald Man*, the *Heap*, or *Sorites*[9] reveals 'the essential vagueness of our common expressions;'[10] and the *Horned Man*[11] seems to be a case of the Aristotelian fallacy of Many Questions.

Two sophisms seem to be of Chrysippean origin, the Wagon and the Nobody, and their flaws seem to be exposed by reference to the Stoic theory of language. The Wagon is:

(1) If you say something, it passes through your mouth.
(2) You say *wagon*.
∴ (3) A wagon passes through your mouth.[12]

Although we would say that this amusing fallacy arises from the confusion of use and mention, Chrysippus may have explained

---

variant formulas. Aulus Gellius states it as follows: 'When I lie and admit that I lie, do I lie or speak the truth?' (*Noctes Atticae* 18. 2. 10, Loeb translation).

[6] Kneale and Kneale, p. 114.
[7] Lucian, in *Vitarum Auctio* 22, expounds the Electra as follows:
   (1) Electra knows her brother Orestes.
   (2) Electra does not know the man standing near her.
   (3) Orestes is the man standing near her.
   ∴ (4) Electra knows and does not know her brother.
[8] Aristotle gives an example similar to the Electra at *Soph. El.* 24. 179^{b}1-4. About the Electra Aristotle might say that 'to be the man standing near Electra" is only an accident of Orestes, not Orestes himself, and the fallacy arises from predicating a property of Orestes, namely, 'being known by Electra to be her brother,' of one of Orestes' accidents. Hence, for Aristotle, the Electra would seem to be a case of Accident. For Quine, on the other hand, the puzzle in the Electra might be due to the substitution of a singular term ('Orestes') by a codesignative term ('the man standing near Electra') in an opaque construction—namely, in (1). Such substitution in an opaque context will not always preserve the truth value of the containing sentence. See Quine (*Word and Object*), p. 151.
[9] At *Academica* 2, 16. 49. Cicero reports that the Sorites is as follows: 'If two is few, then three is few, and four is few, and so on up to ten. Thus, if two is few, ten is few.' According to Horace in *Epistulae* 2. 1. 45, the Bald Man and Heap are respectively: 'Adding one hair at a time, when does a man cease to be bald, and taking away one grain of sand at a time, when does it cease to be a heap.'
[10] Kneale and Kneale, p. 114.
[11] Diog. Laert. (7. 187) reports the Horned Man to be: 'If you never lost something, you have it still; but you never lost horns, ergo you have horns.' (Loeb translation).
[12] Diog. Laert. 7. 187.

it as a confusion of the referents of 'wagon.' In (2) it is the σημαῖνον, the significans, the sound,[13] whereas in (3) the referent of 'wagon' is a nonlinguistic object.[14] Such a sophism raises the sort of problems in language which the Stoic theory is designed to solve.[15]

The other sophism that Chrysippus exclusively is reported to have proposed is the Nobody:

(1) If someone is in Megara, he is not in Athens.
(2) There is a man (ἄνθρωπός ἐστι) in Megara.
∴ (3) There is no man (οὐκ ἐστὶν ἄνθρωπος) in Athens.[16]

My conjecture is that the Stoics postulated their 'third kind' of ambiguity (in part) as an explanation for the difficulty exemplified in this sophism. In fact, they illustrate this kind of ambiguity by 'ἄνθρωπός ἐστιν'[17] ('man is'), which occurs in (2) above. Although this type of ambiguity is examined below,[18] for the present it suffices to say that there is at least a prima facie meeting here of the Stoic discussions of fallacy and ambiguity.

For better or worse, Galen is the major doxographer of the Stoic teaching on ambiguity. But that is not to say that the non-Galenic doxographical tradition provides no information on this subject. For example, Diogenes Laertius informs us that for the Stoics the study of ambiguity falls under the heading Dialectic.[19] Aulus Gellius reports that Chrysippus holds *every* word to be naturally ambiguous, 'since two or more things may be understood from the same word.'[20] But this claim seems to describe a psychological fact about the use of words—namely, that like any signs they may be misunderstood or misassociated with that of which they are truly signs. The semantic notion of ambiguity

---

[13] As a word, 'wagon' is τὸ σημαῖνον, the significans, which is sound (φωνή). See Sextus Empiricus *Adversus Mathematicos* 8. 11-12.
[14] The word 'wagon' refers to a wagon, the object signified for the Stoics. Their term for 'referent' is τυγχάνον. See Sext. Emp. *Adv. Math.* 8. 12.
[15] Their general theory distinguishes φωνή, λεκτόν = πρᾶγμα, and τυγχάνον, or sound, sense, and referent.
[16] Diog. Laert. 7. 187.
[17] See 106,12-14.
[18] See *infra* pp. 65-66.
[19] Diog. Laert. 7. 44.
[20] Aulus Gellius *Noctes Atticae* 11. 12. 1. (Loeb trans.); also SVF II, #152. It is clear that Chrysippus brings up the notion of ambiguity in places other than his treatises especially devoted to the subject; e.g., in his treatise Λογικὰ ζητήματα, where the expression 'ἀμφιβόλους τὰς λέξεις λέγειν,' occurs. See SVF II, #298 (p. 107, ll. 30-31).

may be specified independently of this psychological fact. It assumes that for a person who knows a language L and who does *not* misunderstand (or misperceive) a word w of L, that w is ambiguous if and only if it admits of more than one meaning (expressible in a paraphrase of w).

One description of this semantic notion is preserved in the Stoic general 'definition' of ambiguity: [21]

> ambiguity is discourse (λέξις) signifying two or even more things (πράγματα), signifying them verbally (λεκτικῶς), strictly (κυρίως), and in conformity with the same usage, so that at the same time this discourse may be taken in several senses.[22]

Presumably the force of 'verbally' [23] is to restrict the notion of ambiguity to ambiguity in spoken language (i.e., speech) and other evidence supports the view that the Stoics (unlike Galen) take language to be primarily a phonological rather than an orthographical phenomenon.[24] Furthermore, 'strictly' [25] excludes such cases as 'triangle' from being considered ambiguous, for it is possible that someone understand by 'triangle' a square, but clearly, 'square' is not one of the meanings or paraphrase values of 'triangle'. The example that follows the Stoic definition of ambiguity is 'Αὐλητρὶς πέπτωκε,' which is said to mean both 'a court has fallen three times,' and 'a flute-girl has fallen.' [26] For Galen, of course, this is clearly a case of Combination and Division.

Having exploited the doxographical tradition as far as possible without Galen's assistance, I now turn to Galen's description of the Stoic teaching. As a caveat the reader should be aware of the pitfalls to which the commentator is liable by relying so heavily on one doxographer, Galen, for the purpose of reconstructing

---

[21] Again, the Stoics' general word for ambiguity is ἀμφιβολία.

[22] Diocles of Magnesia (first century B.C. doxographer) in Diog. Laert. 7. 62, (also SVF III, #24, p. 214, ll. 5-10, my translation). von Arnim's ascription of this definition to Diogenes of Babylonia (a follower of Chrysippus) does not appear to have textual warrant.

[23] 'Verbally' is my rendering of 'λεκτικῶς,' and this seems to be its sole occurrence in the Stoic doxography.

[24] For example, the Stoics define a sentence (or language) λόγος, as 'significant sound emitted by the mind,' at Diog. Laert. 7. 56; and, according to Galen, the Stoics fail to recognize ambiguity of accent, which nearly always occurs in written rather than spoken language.

[25] For more on the meaning of 'strictly' ('κυρίως') see *infra* p. 62.

[26] Diog. Laert. 7. 62. A similar example occurs at 100,10 and in Galen's description of the Stoic theory at 106,10.

the Stoic doctrine on this topic. He may be misled by distortion of the teaching present in the doxographical account, a result of the doctrine's being filtered through the prism of the doxographer's own conceptual scheme. And there is no doubt that Galen has strong commitments to such a scheme, his own theory of ambiguity. Furthermore, the commentator may be deceived as to the nature of the Stoic teaching because of the polemical intent of the doxographer in selecting what he does of the teaching that he knows. And it is clear that Galen uses the Stoic enumeration of the kinds of ambiguity as an inductive proof of his own theory, and as an example of a haphazard and unsystematic account of ambiguity in contrast to his own.[27] Although Galen is not known for willfully misrepresenting the teaching of his predecessors,[28] there is no doubt that he is guilty of honest misunderstanding and misrepresentation of previous views.[29] In addition, the commentator faces the handicap of a severely corrupt text—Chapter 4 of *De Captionibus*. With such considerations in mind, an attempt will be made here to use Galen as our witness in reconstructing the Stoic teaching on ambiguity.

In general, the Stoic doctrine amounts to a classification (under eight headings) of the types of ambiguity that occur in the Greek language. Although betraying acuteness in their observation of language, the Stoic theory is marred (on Galen's account) by a fair amount of overlap between the kinds of ambiguity that are specified. The Stoic headings do not seem to be jointly exhaustive and mutually exclusive like Galen's: the Stoics appear to sacrifice the symmetry and elegance of the Galenic classification (which of course was written nearly four centuries later) because they were simply concerned with identifying and describing the sorts of ambiguity that they found most interesting (both logically and linguistically). Given Galen's account of the Stoic teaching, I suggest that the Stoics did not even pretend to be expounding a theory based on the application of classificatory principles. Rather their enterprise consisted in perspicacious observation of this linguistic phenomenon, case by case, with corresponding

---

[27] See 106,1-4 and 108,11-14.

[28] Sextus Empiricus is an example of a doxographer who experiences lapses of intellectual honesty and conscience. See Kneale and Kneale, pp. 117, 142.

[29] See *supra* p. 21.

characterization and enumeration of the kinds they managed to discern.

According to Galen, the more subtle Stoics [30] postulate the following kinds of ambiguity: (1) Common, (2) Simple Homonymy, (3) Compound Homonymy, (4) Ellipsis, (5) Pleonasm, (6) Insignificant Part Construal, (7) Significant Part Construal, and (8) Referability. Galen states that the Stoics fail to recognize apparent ambiguity and Accent [31] (110,10-13), and it appears that Galen would classify the Stoics' kinds under the following headings of his own:

Galenic modes	Corresponding Stoic Kinds
1. Homonymy	(2) Simple Homonymy
	(4) Ellipsis, (5) Pleonasm
2. Amphiboly	(3) Compound Homonymy
	(8) Referability
3. Accent	- - - -
4. Combination and Division	(1) Common, (6) Insignificant Part Construal, (7) Significant Part Construal
5. Form of expression (L)	- - - -
6. Form of expression (S)	- - - -

Upon reflection, however, it seems that certain of the Stoic kinds listed above are misclassified by Galen—namely, Common and Pleonasm. In the following, the eight Stoic kinds will be described and interpreted.

There is no question about the second kind of ambiguity posited by the Stoics, i.e., Simple Homonymy. I have termed it 'simple' in that it occurs in simple or single terms (106,11); namely, in homonyms. Presumably the Stoics would say that a sentence whose ambiguity arises from the occurrence of a homonym is a case of Simple Homonymy. The example they give of a homonym, 'manly,' means both 'of a man' and 'courageous' (106,12).

Galen apparently believes that the fourth kind of Stoic ambiguity, Ellipsis, also corresponds to his mode Homonymy, and according to Galen's account, Ellipsis would in fact be a subspecies of the Stoics' second kind, Simple Homonymy. Hence, on Galen's

---

[30] See *infra* pp. 132-33. Most likely these men are Chrysippus and Diogenes of Babylonia.

[31] Since ambiguity of accent almost never occurs in speech, the Stoic omission of this mode of ambiguity suggests strongly that their analysis is of spoken language exclusively.

view, the separate postulation of Ellipsis is a clear case of redundancy in the Stoic theory. But Galen's opinion to the contrary, the Stoic identification of this kind of ambiguity seems to reveal subtle insight into a linguistic phenomenon, ambiguity of a construction, which is not a case of homonymy at all, but rather of syntactic ambiguity.

Galen's description of this Stoic kind is brief, and there is some textual corruption. Nevertheless, an example of Ellipsis provided by the Stoics would appear to be the sentence 'The son is yours' (106,15). Because the mediating term is lacking, 'yours' is ambiguous between meaning 'of you as his father' and 'of you as his master' (106,15-16). The omission of the term mediating between 'of you' and 'the son' causes the meaning of this pronoun to be obscure.

Ellipsis seems to be exemplified in the following fallacy expounded by Aristotle:

(1) *A* is yours.
(2) *A* is a child.
∴ (3) *A* is your child.[32]

Probably arguing against the Megarians, Aristotle denies that the fallacy turns on the ambiguity of 'yours' in premise (1). He reasons that an ambiguous term strictly and literally means more than one thing, whereas 'yours' does not. For 'No one speaks of *A* as being '*B*'s child' in the literal sense, if *B* is the child's master.'[33] Aristotle classifies this sophism under the heading Accident.[34] According to Galen's report, the Stoics would seem to oppose Aristotle on the analysis of this argument and would affirm that it is a case of ambiguity of Ellipsis.

I suggest that the following analysis of Ellipsis explains how it is ambiguity, but not homonymy. It is based on the fact that in Greek, the possessive pronoun 'σός' ('your') and the genitive of the personal pronoun 'σοῦ' ('yours'), are equivalent.[35] The former occurs both in the example at 106,15 and in Aristotle's sophism that is cited above. What is ambiguous about 'yours' (or 'Picasso's', to use a non-deictic or nontoken-reflexive term) is its construction. The genitive case in which it falls is either a genitive of ownership possession or a genitive of inalienable pos-

---

[32] *Soph. El.* 24. 180ª4-6.
[33] *Soph. El.* 24. 180ª2-4, (Oxford translation).
[34] *Soph. El.* 24. 180ª4, and see *supra* p. 20, n. 19.
[35] Smyth (*Greek Grammar*) p. 299, sec. 1196.

session [36] (including kinship relations). And the ellipsis or omission of a mediating term preserves the ambiguity of the genitive construction.

If the mediating term is 'master,' then the sentence 'the son is yours' may be paraphrased, 'the son is your slave' or equivalently, 'you are the son's master.' In this case, the ambiguity of the genitive is resolved in favor of the genitive of ownership possession. But if the mediating term is 'father,' then the sentence in question may be paraphrased, 'you are the son's father,' the ambiguity of the genitive being resolved in favor of the genitive of inalienable possession. The key point here is that the ambiguity of Ellipsis is a result of the ambiguity of the possessive pronoun or genitive construction, not of 'your' per se. The ambiguity occurs because of the syntax, a term's being in the genitive case (or its equivalent), rather than of the word itself (e.g., the pronoun 'you' in the nominative case).

This interpretation of Ellipsis, as a form of syntactic ambiguity, makes plain how the Stoics might have analyzed the fallacy Aristotle discussed that is described above.[37] In premise (1) 'yours' is taken as equivalent to a genitive of ownership possession, and the premise as a whole may be paraphrased 'you are A's master,' 'master' being the mediating term that is omitted. But in the conclusion (3), 'your' is read as equivalent to a genitive of inalienable possession, and the conclusion may be paraphrased 'You are father to child A,' 'father' being the mediating term that is omitted. And it is precisely the ellipsis or omission of these mediating terms that preserves the ambiguity of the genitive construction and of the sentences in which it occurs.[38]

The seeming converse of Ellipsis for the Stoics is Pleonasm, and Galen presumably also classifies this kind of ambiguity under his heading Homonymy. Superfluity (rather than omission) of words produces the ambiguity in a case of Pleonasm (or Redundancy). In a pleonastic sentence, the ambiguity arises from the occurrence of a redundant word, one not necessary to the sense of the sentence, but whose inclusion is dictated by linguistic

---

[36] This terminology is that of Charles J. Fillmore, in 'A Case for Case,' in *Universals in Linguistic Theory*, ed. by E. Bach and R. T. Harms (New York: Holt, Rinehart and Winston, 1968), p. 61.

[37] See *supra* p. 62.

[38] On this analysis of Ellipsis, it corresponds to Galen's mode Amphiboly (actual, syntactic ambiguity), rather than Homonymy.

convention. In their description of this fifth kind of ambiguity, the Stoics identify what grammarians have since called the 'redundant μή.' [39] The 'μή' ('not') in the Stoic example ('He forbade him (not) to sail,' 106,17), either negates the infinitive or it does not. If 'μή' is construed with the infinitive, then 'μή' is a genuine sign of negation, and the infinitive is negated. But if 'μή' is construed with the sentence operator (or main verb) 'forbid,' then it is a weak form of negation, which functions not to negate the infinitive but merely to emphasize the negative idea of 'forbidding,' that is, telling someone *not* to do something. On this interpretation, Pleonasm falls under Galen's heading Amphiboly, not Homonymy. In a case of Pleonasm, what may be *construed* in more than one way is, on one reading, redundant to the meaning of the sentence.

Both the third kind of Stoic ambiguity, 'Compound Homonymy,' and the eighth, 'Referability,' also seem to fall under the Galenic heading Amphiboly. But on closer scrutiny, only Referability seems to qualify as syntactic ambiguity 'in the fuller sense ... of what is syntactically connected with what,'[40] whereas Compound Homonymy seems rather to be a case of the lesser form of syntactic ambiguity, ambiguity of constructions.[41] First, however, the discussion turns to Referability.

A sentence which is ambiguous due to Referability 'fails to make clear what refers to what' (108,8); that is, how its constituents are to be construed. In both examples that Galen reports the Stoics give for Referability, the ambiguity arises from the juxtaposition of nouns in the same grammatical case, either of which may assume the grammatical role (subject or object) of the other.[42] One of the examples resembles Galen's example of Amphiboly at 88,11.[43] The other example, 'ΔΙΩΝΘΕΩΝΕΣΤΙΝ,' ('Dion Theon is') is on one reading said to refer to the existence of both Dion and Theon, in which case both nouns (in the nominative case) are construed as subjects of the verb 'is.' As such, the sentence may be rendered 'Dion (and) Theon exist.' On the other hand, the

---

[39] See Smyth, p. 622, sec. 2739.
[40] Quine (*Word and Object*), p. 135.
[41] *Ibid*. As we have seen, Ellipsis seems to be an example of such syntactic ambiguity. See *supra* pp. 62-63.
[42] It is assumed here that Referability is one of the Stoic kinds that Galen terms 'Syntactic Homonymy' at 110,6-9.
[43] The example at 110,8-9 may be rendered 'May Socrates prevail over Meletus' and 'May Meletus prevail over Socrates.'

sentence in question may refer to the identity of these men. In that case 'Dion' is construed as grammatical subject, and 'Theon' as part of the predicate, or vice versa: 'Dion is Theon' or 'Theon is Dion.'

Similar to Referability in corresponding to the Galenic mode Amphiboly, is 'Homonymy in Compounds of Words,' which I term 'Compound Homonymy.' Here, as in the case of Ellipsis, it seems that the Stoics are identifying ambiguity of constructions, rather than of syntactic *construals* (although construction ambiguity is syntactic ambiguity).[44] The example provided, 'ἄνθρωπός ἐστιν'[45] ('man is') seems to be a case of a construction, which, depending on the linguistic environment in which it occurs, admits of more than one reading. Consider 'ἄνθρωπός ἐστιν' (or 'ἔστιν ἄνθρωπος,' the word order being irrelevant), as part of a sentence frame with two gaps:

_____ ἄνθρωπός ἐστιν _____

If the first gap remains empty and the second is filled in with 'ἐν Μεγάροις,' ('in Megara'), then the sentence may be rendered 'A man is in Megara.' That is, 'a particular man is in Megara'— hence, the Stoic explanation that 'ἄνθρωπός ἐστιν' may signify the being of a particular case (πτῶσις);[46] i.e., a particular man. And this I take to be the second premise of the Nobody sophism specified above.[47]

However, when the first gap is filled in with 'οὐκ,' the sign of negation, and the second gap is filled in with 'in Megara,' (and the positions of 'ἄνθρωπος' and 'ἐστίν' are reversed), then the sentence has an entirely different sense. It does not read 'A particular man is not in Megara,' but rather 'No man is in Megara.' In this case, the construction 'ἔστιν ἄνθρωπος' refers not to a particular man, but to the being of the essence Man, the extension of which is the class of men—none of this essence is present in Megara.

---

[44] See Quine (*Word and Object*), pp. 134-35. Consider the word 'parrot' in English, and assume it is unambiguous, and means 'psittacine animal.' But the construction 'a parrot' *is* ambiguous, and I suggest may be analyzed as a case of Compound Homonymy. For in the sentence, 'A parrot likes to say my name,' the indefinite singular term 'a parrot' means 'some parrot.' But in the sentence, 'A parrot is brightly feathered,' 'a parrot' means 'every parrot.'

[45] See 106,13.

[46] See 106,14 and *infra* pp. 133-34 on this use of 'πτῶσις.'

[47] See *supra* p. 58, and Diog. Lart. 7. 187.

Hence, the Stoics say that 'ἄνθρωπός ἐστιν' may also signify the being (in this case, the non-being) of the essence Man.[48] And I propose that it is by reference to this kind of ambiguity that the Stoics expose the fallacy of the Nobody sophism. Clearly, the conclusion warranted is 'A particular man is not in Athens,' not 'No man is in Athens,' although both of these conclusions may be expressed by the same sentence in Greek. The absence of a theory of quantification and negation adequate to deal with such sophisms seems to be (in part) responsible for the Stoics' reliance on a species of ambiguity, Compound Homonymy, to explain the puzzle.[49]

There is little difficulty in understanding the Stoics' sixth and seventh kinds of ambiguity, which are respectively 'Insignificant Part Construal' and 'Significant Part Construal.' They comfortably fall under the Galenic mode, Combination and Division. In fact, the example Galen provides for the Stoic seventh kind is the same example he gives of his own mode Combination and Division.[50] Significant Part Construal arises from the disposition of a significant expression in a sentence to be construed in two or more ways, and its ambiguity is of a sort that is mechanically resolved by the distinct placement of word break (pause) in speech. Insignificant Part Construal is the ambiguity that occurs when insignificant parts of a sentence, (for the Stoics, letters, syllables, and connectives),[51] can be construed in more than one way when the sentence is uttered, and such ambiguity is also easily resolved by the me-

---

[48] See 106,14. If this use of 'οὐσία' does not sound Stoic, but rather Aristotelian, we must remember that this word choice may be an interpolation on Galen's part. For the Stoics, 'οὐσία' is either prime matter which neither increases nor diminishes, or finite matter. See Diog. Laert. 7. 150.

[49] An alternative interpretation of this kind of ambiguity is one along the same lines as that proposed for Referability. For the example given, one might say that its syntactic ambiguity lies in the disposition of 'ἄνθρωπος' to function either as subject or predicate. In the first case, the sentence may be rendered, 'Man is,' and in the second, 'He is a man'; i.e., a particular entity is a man. But on this account, Compound Homonymy is not different in kind, only in degree of complexity, from Referability. Moreover, there is no connection with the Nobody. Hence, it is a less attractive interpretation than the one proposed in the text.

[50] See 88,18 and *Soph. El.* 4. 166ᵃ37-38.

[51] Unlike the other parts of speech, the connective is not said to signify or to indicate anything, only to join the other parts. Connectives are described as indeclinable parts of speech (Diog. Laert. 7. 57-58). But it is clear from Diog. Laert. 7. 69, 71-75, that connectives link together simple ἀξιώματα into complex ἀξιώματα.

chanical addition of pauses. In the example given, a letter, η,⁵² may be construed as the last letter of one word ('κενή,' 'void'), the first letter of another word ('ἧπαρ', 'liver'), and as a disjunctive connective ('ἤ,' 'or').⁵³

More controversial is the Stoics' fourth kind of ambiguity, 'Common.' It is said to be the sort of ambiguity that is common to a single word and to two words,⁵⁴ presumably both of which are pronounced the same, like 'αὐλητρίς' and 'αὐλὴ τρίς,' ('flute-girl' and 'court three times'). Now Galen assumes that this Stoic ambiguity corresponds to his own mode, Combination and Division; at least this is the mode under which his example 'αὐλητρίς' falls. But there seems some reason to believe that for the Stoics, this example is common in the sense that it falls under two other kinds of ambiguity; namely, Simple Homonymy and Compound Homonymy. That is, as one phonological unit (describable as one word), 'αὐλητρίς' means both 'flute-girl' and 'court three times,' so it is a case of Simple Homonymy. But the same phonological unit (describable as two words), 'αὐλὴ τρίς' also has these two meanings, and hence is a case of Compound Homonymy, a construction which is ambiguous, like 'man is.' If this is the case, then it is clear that the Stoics would disagree with Galen's subsumption of this example under the mode Combination and Division, a type of ambiguity that is neatly resolved by the mechanics of pause. The Stoic denial of this for the illustration at hand suggests that 'αὐλητρίς' and 'αὐλὴ τρίς' were, under normal conditions, pronounced in the same way ⁵⁵ (and hence, the ambiguity really is common to the articulate sound, whether thought of abstractly as one word or two). Moreover, it suggests that the

---

⁵² A letter is primarily a sound, (η is one of the φωνήεντα or vowels,) though a letter is also a written character. See Diog. Laert. 7. 56-57.

⁵³ See 108,1-4. At Diog. Laert. 7. 72, a disjunction is said to be composed by means of the disjunctive connective 'or.' This connective announces that one of the ἀξιώματα it connects is false. On this, see Kneale and Kneale, pp. 147-49.

⁵⁴ See 106,8-11.

⁵⁵ Presumably neither expression was pronounced with pause. and according to Carl D. Buck, in *Comparative Grammar of Greek and Latin* (Chicago: University of Chicago Press, 1933), p. 163, 'All syllables not having the acute or the circumflex, that is, what we call unaccented syllables, were regarded as having the grave.' Hence, the spoken accents are identical in 'αὐλητρίς' and 'αὐλὴ τρίς.' Here the Stoic criterion of the identity of discourse is suggested: two bits of discourse are identical when they have the same phonological value.

Galenic strategy of appropriating so-called 'compound' words under the heading Combination and Division is indeed an ad hoc and artificial move,[56] designed to accommodate compound words to Galen's rigid lexical-syntactic division.

In sum, despite the difficulties that threaten to prevent a systematic discussion of the Stoic teaching on ambiguity, there is some reason to believe that Galen's account has now been sufficiently de-Galenized to serve as a reputable basis on which to reconstruct the Stoic doctrine. We find that the Stoics seem to be at least partially motivated in their studies of ambiguity by the desire to explain certain sophisms. Moreover, the evidence points to the fact that the Stoics are concerned with ambiguity in *speech* (rather than in written language), and that their descriptions of the types of ambiguity were produced in a philosophical environment which was free from commitments to a fixed set of taxonomic principles (as Galen's theory clearly was not). Their description of Ellipsis and their identification of 'Compound Homonymy' speak for their insight into certain elusive forms of ambiguity. Their discovery of the 'redundant μή' reflects their critical acumen in the field of grammar and language in general. Though we have but a few pages of summary for detailed studies that filled many volumes, the glimpses we are allowed make it obvious that the Stoics acquit themselves admirably on the subject of ambiguity in language.

---

[56] See 100,6-11 and *infra* pp. 129-30.

CHAPTER EIGHT

SYNOPTIC ANALYSIS OF *DE CAPTIONIBUS* [1]

In the first part of Chapter 1 of *De Captionibus* Galen illustrates and briefly characterizes what he takes to be the six Aristotelian modes of ambiguity [2] that cause and denominate the six corresponding fallacies *in dictione*—Homonymy, Amphiboly, Accent, Combination, Division, and Form of expression. That is, he specifies the connection between ambiguity and fallacy as it has been set by Aristotle's analysis. Contrary to our initial impression, however, this chapter does not form the prelude to another commentary on Aristotelian logic. Galen's goal is not to defend or to improve upon the Aristotelian classification of the types of ambiguity, but to formulate a true theory of ambiguity. Presumably Galen takes Aristotle's enumeration of the modes of ambiguity to be largely correct, so correct in fact that it becomes a natural point of departure for Galen's own theory of ambiguity.

Galen's condensed description of the Aristotelian modes of ambiguity is wayward, however, in that it assumes that Accent, Combination, and Division are cases of ambiguity (whereas they are for Aristotle cases of linguistic confusion), and it treats Combination and Division as one mode. Otherwise, it is a fair (albeit abbreviated) account of Aristotle. For example, a sentence is said to be a case of Homonymy when its ambiguity results from the ambiguity of (at least) one of its words, a homonym. Galen's example of a homonym, 'κύων' ('dog,' 'dogstar,' 'Cynic philosopher') is straight from Aristotle.[3]

Galen describes a case of Amphiboly as a sentence which is ambiguous as a sentence, although none of its words is ambiguous (88,10-12). This characterization is about as imprecise as Aristotle's own, which states that a case of Amphiboly occurs when

---

[1] I wish to apologize here for the amount of repetition of points made earlier to be found in this synopsis. The summary of the argument is designed primarily as an explication for those puzzlied by Galen's text or the corresponding translation, and it does not assume a careful reading of previous chapters in the Introduction.
[2] See *supra* pp. 20-28.
[3] *Soph. El.* 4. 166^{a}16.

there is a sentence, the words of which when taken in isolation are univocal, but when taken together are ambiguous.[4] What both Galen and Aristotle have recognized is structural or grammatical ambiguity, but neither seems to have the terminology adequate to articulate that a sentence is amphibolous when one or more of its words (each with only one sense) can assume more than one grammatical role; e.g., be subject or object of an infinitive. In an amphibolous sentence, its grammar or structure causes it to admit of two readings, and hence the sentence is ambiguous.

Galen mistakenly describes the Aristotelian mode Accent as a case of a sentence which is *ambiguous* due to the accentuation (including breathings) of one of its words (88,13-15).[5] That is, Galen interprets Aristotle as claiming that in a case of Accent, one word (in a sentence) like 'ορος' has two senses, depending on whether it is taken as 'ὅρος' or 'ὄρος'; i.e., with a rough breathing at the beginning or not. On this interpretation, Accent appears to become a species of Homonymy. But in the theory he introduces in Chapter 3, Galen holds that Accent is in fact a kind of ambiguity coordinate with Homonymy.

As mentioned above, Galen treats the modes Combination and Division as one, stating that a sentence which is a case of Combination and Division is ambiguous when that sentence may be grammatically construed with certain of its constituents either combined or divided.[6] The example Galen gives of Combination and Division is identical with one that Aristotle includes as a case of Division.[7] It may be paraphrased as 'Noble Achilles left fifty of a hundred men,' and 'Noble Achilles left a hundred of fifty men,' (88,18). Although the second reading is numerically impossible, it is a possible translation of the sentence. We recall that in some of Aristotle's examples of ambiguity, one of the dual meanings is absurd;[8] so we should not be troubled by Galen's and Aristotle's example mentioned above.

---

[4] *Soph. El.* 4. 166ª17-18.

[5] For Aristotle, a case of Accent is not a case of ambiguity, but of taking a sentence with a word accented in one way for a sentence which is the same as the first except that it contains a word accented in another way.

[6] Strictly speaking, for Aristotle Combination and Division are cases of linguistic confusion, not of ambiguity. See *supra* pp. 24-28.

[7] *Soph. El.* 4. 166ª37-38.

[8] At *Soph. El.* 4. 166ª18-21 Aristotle tolerates a nonsensical construal of the example of Amphiboly, 'ἐπίσταται γράμματα,' in which the word 'γράμματα' functions either as object or subject—'He has knowledge of letters' or 'Letters have knowledge.'

Galen's description of Form of expression is faithful to Aristotle's account. Galen tells us that this mode of ambiguity occurs when a word appears to signify one thing (or, appears to have one logic) on account of the form in which it is expressed, whereas it in fact signifies something else (or, has a different logic). For example, the one word sentence 'ἀκούω' ('I hear') in fact signifies a passivity, but because of the form in which it is expressed (a form similar to verbs specifying a different logical category, namely 'activity'), it *appears* to signify an activity.

Having briefly surveyed what he takes to be the six Aristotelian modes of ambiguity, Galen cites a passage in *Sophistici Elenchi* in which Aristotle states that there are both inductive and deductive proofs to show that the six fallacies (which fall under, and are caused and denominated by the modes of ambiguity) are jointly exhaustive:

> To show this, there is a proof by induction and a syllogism, (and perhaps there is some other syllogism that may be taken), that this is the number of ways in which we may fail to mean the same thing by the same words and sentences.[9]

Galen briefly specifies the conditions of an inductive proof which shows that the list of fallacies *in dictione* is exhaustive (90,13-16), and questions whether any deductive proof (syllogism) can be brought forth other than the one Aristotle is suggesting.[10] Galen perversely seems to construe the last clause of the above passage, 'that this is the number of ways in which we may fail to mean the same thing by the same words and sentences,' as being in apposition with the first occurrence of the word 'syllogism' in the same sentence. Reading it in this way, Galen accuses Aristotle of providing a syllogistic conclusion in the above rather than a complete syllogism (90,20-22). But Galen immediately absolves Aristotle from this error, by reference to Aristotle's frequent use of signs, and brevity in general, when he is writing for those who have already heard the explanation (90,22-92,1). Galen blames Aristotle's brevity for preventing commentators from interpreting this passage satisfactorily.

Galen concludes Chapter 1 on a methodological note. He proposes

---

[9] *Soph. El.* 4. 165^{b}27-30, and 90,10-13.
[10] Galen specifies what this syllogism might be at 104,2-5. See *infra* pp. 79-80.

to be precise about these matters, not for the sake of Aristotle, but rather for his own sake and presumably for the sake of discovering the truth about them (92,3-4). It is the mark of a philosopher, Galen observes, not only to draw inferences when certain premises are given, but also to adduce the appropriate premises when confronted with a certain conclusion (92,5-7). Here the conclusion in question is, 'that this is the number of ways we may fail to mean the same thing by the same words and sentences.' In Chapter 3 Galen accepts the challenge and does in fact construct the premises of this conclusion. But Galen does so, not as an Aristotelian commentator, but as an independent philosopher whose own theory happens to support the canonical Aristotelian doctrine. It is clear that Galen is not interested simply in expounding and interpreting Aristotle, and he says so himself at 92,3-4. Rather Galen's use of the Aristotelian material is largely heuristic, designed to provide a framework for the development of Galen's own teaching.

At the beginning of *Chapter* 2 Galen sums up the task at hand, which is to show that the fallacies [11] due to language are as many in number as the fallacies due to ambiguity on Aristotle's account. We recall that Galen (mistakenly) reads Aristotle as postulating six types of fallacy due to ambiguity, so Galen's project is in effect to show that the fallacies due to language are six in number. He maintains that the proof of this rests on two premises:

(1) Every fallacy (kind) due to language is a fallacy due to ambiguity (92,10-11).
(2) There are six kinds of fallacy due to ambiguity (92,11).

These premises together with the following trivial and implicit assumption,

(3) Every fallacy (kind) due to ambiguity is a fallacy due to language

entail what Galen is seeking to prove, namely

(4) There are six kinds of fallacy due to language.

The structure of this inference may be rendered more perspicuous if expressed in set theoretical terms. Accordingly, (2) may be paraphrased as 'The set or class of fallacy (kinds) due to ambiguity

---

[11] In this discussion, 'fallacy' will specify a fallacy-kind, of which particular fallacies committed in discourse are cases.

has six members,' and the conjunction of (1) and (3) as 'the class of fallacy (kinds) due to ambiguity is extensionally equivalent to the class of fallacy (kinds) due to language; that is, these classes have the same members.' It follows immediately from (2) with (1) and (3) that the class of fallacy (kinds) due to language has six members, which may be reformulated as (4)—there are six kinds of fallacy due to language. Galen establishes premise (1) in this chapter, and leaves until Chapter 3 the consideration of premise (2).

To establish (1) Galen trots out a complex argument and its corresponding conceptual apparatus.[12] The immediate argument for (1) is found at the end of Chapter 2, and it is as follows:

    (a) Every fallacy due to language is a fallacy due to the (sole) vice of language (96,19-20).
    (b) Ambiguity is the (sole) vice of language (96,18).
∴ (1) Every fallacy (kind) due to language is a fallacy due to ambiguity (92,10-11 and 96,20-21).

(a) is never argued for by Galen, so it presumably qualifies as an obviously true principle for him based on his observation of sophists (92,13-14). What needs argument is (b), and Galen provides two independent arguments for it. The first may be reconstructed as follows:

    (c) The function of language is signifying (92,21-22; 94,9-10).
    (d) The virtue of language lies in its function and consists in its performing its function well (92,20).
∴ (e) The virtue of language is signifying well.
    (f) Vice (of language) is the failure (or negation) of the corresponding virtue (92,17-18).
∴ (g) The vice of language is either not signifying or not signifying well (94,11).
    (h) If x is the vice of language, then fallacy due to language results from x (92,11-13).
    (i) But no fallacy due to language results from language which does not signify (which has no meaning at all), (96,5-7).
∴ (j) It is not the case that the vice of language is not signifying (from (h) and (i)).
∴ (k) The vice of language is not signifying well (from conjunction of (j) and (g), 96,7).

---

[12] That is, Galen brings in the concepts of the function of language, and of the *vice* of language, which is the failure of its *virtue*.

(m) Not signifying well is signifying ambiguously, that is, ambiguity (96,8).
∴ (b) The vice of language is ambiguity (96,18).

Premise (c) above is at the heart of Galen's theory of language, and requires no argument. (d) seems to be an application of a Platonic and Aristotelian principle,[13] though Galen gives these philosophers no credit for it. Slightly problematic is (g). For if the virtue of language is signifying well, then it would follow that the vice of language is not signifying well. The disjunction results presumably from the ambiguity as to what the 'not' ('μή') operates on. If it operates on 'signifying' then 'not signifying well' means it does not signify, but if it operates on 'well' then 'not signifying well' means 'signifying not well' or 'signifying poorly.'[14]

Galen argues for (i), claiming rightly that no one would accept or propose a premise in language that means nothing at all (96,6-7). And the conjunction of (h) and (i) entails (j). It may be noted that Galen offers another proof for (j) at 94,12-14, where he argues (by analogy with the flute-player) that language which does not signify is not language, and implicitly that not signifying cannot be the vice of language, for what has this vice cannot be language.

Returning to the argument at hand, we find that the conjunction of (j) and (g) entails (k), and that the conjunction of (k) and (m) entails (b). Galen supplies another argument for (b) and he acknowledges that its first premise is straight from Plato.[15] This second argument may be reconstructed as follows:

(s) For any corruptible thing x, if something y corrupts x, then y is the vice of x (96,11-12).
(t) Ambiguity corrupts language in that it produces obscurity with qualification (96,12-13).
∴ (b) Ambiguity is the vice of language (96,15).

Hence, Galen includes two arguments for (b), the second primarily based on an appeal to Plato. By establishing (b) with this double-indemnity protection from error, Galen may infer (1), that every fallacy due to language is a fallacy due to ambiguity.[16]

---

[13] Plato *Respublica* 1. 352D-353C; 10. 601D; Aristotle *Ethica Nicomachea* 1. 7. 1097^{b}24-1098^{a}20.

[14] It may be that the disjunction results from the ambiguity of the expression 'x is in y' (e.g., 'the excellence of language is in signifying'), which may mean 'x is identical with y' or 'x exists in relation to y.' See 94,1 and 94,16-17.

[15] See 96,10-12 and *Resp.* 10. 609a3-609d2.

[16] See *supra* p. 73.

Now that the pattern of argumentation of Chapter 2 has been sketched, I turn to certain related topics which Galen treats in passing. For example, in one excursus at 96,3-6 Galen offers a psychological explanation for someone's believing that the vice of language is the failure to signify (i.e., not signifying) rather than not signifying well. The benighted believer's error springs from his confusing two expressions that resemble one another, 'not signifying' and 'not signifying well.'

A more serious digression takes Galen to the subject of accidental vs. essential virtues (94,1-6). By distinguishing these sorts of virtue Galen makes clear what it means to say that signifying well is the virtue of language per se (i.e., is an essential virtue of language). An essential virtue of a thing is the excellence to be found in that thing's function. It is called an *essential* virtue because the function and the essence of a thing coincide (94,16).

On the other hand, any excellence of a thing that is not found in its function is an accidental virtue. Galen illustrates an accidental virtue by reference to a sword with an ivory hilt. The virtue of having an ivory hilt attaches to the sword *qua* ornamental object, not to the sword *qua* sword, the function of which is to cut (94,4-6). In like manner, an eye which is adorned with eye shadow has an accidental virtue. But only an eye that sees well has its essential virtue, for the function of an eye is to see, not to be a beautiful object (94,4-6).

With regard to language, two of its accidental virtues are sonority and calligraphy, for they are not found in the function of language, signifying. Rather they are excellences of language *qua* spoken sound and *qua* set of inscriptions. The essential virtue of language is signifying well, i.e., with lucidity, and the negation of the essential virtue of language is signifying not well, i.e., ambiguously. The *essential* vice of language then is ambiguity, and it is this with which Galen is concerned in the arguments in this chapter. In this connection, at 94,15-18, Galen denies that elliptical utterance, prolixity, or redundance is a vice of language without qualification (presumably an essential vice of language). They appear to be vices of style rather than vices that are found in the signification of language. Galen admits them as (essential) vices only if they cause ambiguity and obscurity (96,18), which they need not do in every case.

Since he has proved in Chapter 2 that every fallacy due to

language is a fallacy due to ambiguity, in *Chapter 3* Galen announces that his purpose is to show that there are six kinds of fallacy due to ambiguity. These two, we recall, are crucial premises in the argument that there are six kinds of fallacy due to language.[17]

Galen's proofs that there are six kinds of fallacy due to ambiguity are based on an exhaustive division of the notion of sentential ambiguity.[18] This is indicated initially at 98,2-5, where Galen alerts his reader to the fact that the present investigation begins from reflection on what a sentence is and that this inquiry will be into sentential ambiguity.

As a preface to his application of the diairetic method, Galen articulates a preliminary definition of a sentence; to wit, 'a combination of names' (98,5-6). He specifies that among names he is including verbs and 'whatever signifies something,' thereby adopting a convention that conforms with ordinary usage, since 'ὄνομα' ('name') has wide applicability in Greek common parlance.[19] Clearly, Galen's syntactic description of a sentence and its constituents is inadequate for anything other than a rough indication to readers of this introductory treatise of how he is using the term 'λόγος' ('sentence').

Galen next performs his analysis. Given an ambiguous sentence, the ambiguity will be situated in one of the words or in the sentence as such (i.e., in the combination of words, the sentential structure), (98,7-8). That is, sentential ambiguity is either lexical or syntactic. There is no tertium quid (98,8-9). Furthermore, ambiguity is like everything else that exists or is capable of mention. That is, it is actual, potential, or apparent (98,10-12).

Each of the modes enumerated in Chapter 1 will have these properties pairwise—that is, it will be both either lexical or syntactic, and actual, potential, or apparent. Homonymy is said to be actual lexical ambiguity, and Amphiboly, actual syntactic ambiguity. Cases of these modes are said to be *actual* since they in fact (as they stand) have two meanings (98,13-16). Accent is said to be potential lexical ambiguity, and Combination and Division, potential syntactic ambiguity. These latter modes are said to be potential because it is *possible* for a case of them to

---

[17] See 92,10-11 and *supra* p. 72.
[18] See *supra* pp. 49-52.
[19] 'ὄνομα' seems to have the same extension in ordinary Greek as 'word' in English.

signify one of two things, although it in fact signifies only one thing after accentual marks or word divisions have been applied or made. Galen exemplifies the mode Accent with the sentence 'ορος ἕστηκεν,' which *can* mean two distinct things, but whose ambiguity is resolved when accentuation (including aspiration) has been added to 'ορος'.[20]

At this point Galen digresses on the problem of the sentence whose ambiguity is due to the occurrence of a compound word. The issue raised is whether such ambiguity is lexical or syntactic (100,6-11). Galen opts for the latter alternative, and explains that compound words resemble sentences (λόγοι) since they are compounds of words. For example, a sentence with a compound word like 'αὐλητρίς' will be a unit that means 'flute-girl' if it is taken as combined, and a unit that means 'court three times' if it is taken as divided (100,10-11).

At 100,10-11 Galen proceeds to resolve the paradox that Accent, and Combination and Division both cause and cure fallacies due to language. In the first case, they are modes of ambiguity that the sophist trades upon in reasoning fallaciously. In the second case, Accent, and Combination and Division are the processes of adding accentuation and word breaks which resolve the potential ambiguity of such sentences, and hence cure or expose the fallacies in which (as modes of ambiguity) they occur (100,14-15). Clearly the paradox results from the ambiguity of the terms 'Accent,' and 'Combination and Division.'

At this point in the discussion of potential ambiguity, Galen indicates how it generates fallacies. What happens is that the sophist proposes a premise which is potentially ambiguous and assumes it has one meaning, but when he draws his conclusion, he assumes it means something else (100,16-18). By tacitly adding accentuation and word breaks, the sophist 'changes the sentence' but reasons as though it were the same sentence (unaltered by accentuation or word break), (102,1-2). Galen's illustration of the fallacy Combination and Division is poor in that it contains more than one relevant flaw:

(1) Rational is one word.
(2) Rational is a proprium of man.
∴ (3) The Rational one is a proprium of man.

---

[20] See *supra* pp. 44-45, and 100,4-5.

Overlooking the confusion of use and mention in the argument, we may identify the cause of the fallacy as premise (1), which is potentially ambiguous in Greek. For on one placement of pause or punctuation, 'one' is construed as predicate, but on another placement of pause or punctuation (which the sophist tacitly trades on), 'one' is construed as part of the subject. The potential ambiguity is reflected more plainly in the conclusion (3) above, which in Greek may be rendered 'The Rational is one proprium of man' and 'The Rational one is a proprium of man.' Again, the meaning of this sentence depends on where the word break is made, and hence, on how the words are grouped.

The example Galen provides of the fallacy Accent as reconstructed [21] is a clear case of a sophism that depends on the second premise being tacitly changed when the conclusion is drawn. For that premise, 'A ορος does not stand there' may be read both as 'A ὅρος (boundary) does not stand there' and 'A ὄρος (hill) does not stand there.'

Galen admits that no one would be tricked by these obvious examples of fallacies due to potential ambiguity, but that the sophists do the same thing in cases of actual ambiguity where the fraud is less obvious. For cases of Homonymy and Amphiboly, as they stand, might be agreed to with either meaning—their ambiguity is not due to the lack of word break or punctuation.[22] At 102,9-10 Galen reminds his reader that Aristotle said 'we mean different things by the same words and sentences,' because in fact some words and sentences are the same (namely, in cases of actual ambiguity), and the sophists do violence to their form by altering their meaning while at the same time leaving their form undisturbed.

Having made these remarks about potential and actual ambiguity, Galen turns to apparent ambiguity. For examples of this species, Galen refers his readers to the works of Eudemus of Rhodes and to other treatises.[23] Since apparent ambiguity is both lexical and syntactic (102,13-14), it would follow that Form of expression is two modes, which I distinguish with subscripts, as 'Form of expression$_{(L)}$' and 'Form of expression$_{(S)}$.' Hence, Galen's

---

[21] See *infra* pp. 130-31.
[22] See *supra* pp. 41-42.
[23] See *supra* pp. 46.

division of the concept of sentential ambiguity may be depicted on the following matrix:

	Lexical	Syntactic
Actual	Homonymy	Amphiboly
Potential	Accent	Combination and Division
Apparent	Form of expression$_{(L)}$	Form of expression$_{(S)}$

Galen then appears to provide a very condensed direct proof that there are precisely six kinds of ambiguity (102,16-104,1), which may be reconstructed as follows:

(1) If our division of sentential ambiguity is exhaustive, and ambiguity is either lexical or syntactic, and actual, potential, or apparent, then there are six kinds of ambiguity.

(2) Our division of sentential ambiguity is exhaustive and ambiguity is either lexical or syntactic, and actual, potential, or apparent.

∴ (3) There are six kinds of ambiguity.

Galen also maintains that a *reductio ad impossibile* (an indirect proof) can also be constructed for (3) above, as long as this indirect proof embodies the division of sentential ambiguity (104,2). This *reductio* may be formulated as follows:

(a) Assume that (3) is false: that it is not true that there are six kinds of ambiguity, but rather that there is another, a seventh kind (104,3-4).

(b) Any seventh kind of ambiguity will be neither lexical nor syntactic, and not actual, potential, or apparent (104,4-5).

(c) But our account shows no other ambiguity besides these, which contradicts the statement that a seventh kind will be neither lexical nor syntactic, and not actual, potential, or apparent (104,5).

∴ (d) (3) is true: there are six kinds of ambiguity.

If it is assumed (and it seems to be so at 102,16-18,) that the fallacies due to ambiguity are the same in number as the kinds of ambiguity, then it follows immediately that there are six kinds of fallacy due to ambiguity.

Thus, by both direct and indirect proof the division of sentential ambiguity has shown why there are six kinds of fallacy due to ambiguity. The indirect proof for Galen is presumably what Aristotle means by the other syllogism (90,19-20) that can be used to show that there are six fallacies due to ambiguity, and hence, six fallacies due to language.

At 104,5 Galen assumes the role of an orthodox commentator and relates the work done in this chapter to Aristotle's teaching. It is clear that both Galen's and Aristotle's modes of ambiguity (on Galen's (mis)understanding of Aristotle) are *nominally* the same, though Galen joins Aristotle's modes Combination and Division into one mode, and splits Aristotle's mode Form of expression into two modes, one lexical and one syntactic. At any rate, Galen here insists that this application of the method to the notion of sentential ambiguity has disclosed the nature of ambiguity, and that his results do not constitute a procrustean effort to accommodate his theory to Aristotle's doctrine. But Galen also holds that he is not doing Aristotle a favor here, because the Galenic theory is latent in Aristotle, and Galen appears to take credit merely for making Aristotle's views explicit.[24]

Galen states that Aristotle's account is itself methodically written (104,8). For the lexical-syntactic distinction is the Stagirite's, in his remark, 'that we mean different things by the same words and sentences,' (104,8-10). Moreover, Galen indicates that the actual-potential-apparent division may be found in Aristotle's initial discussion of the fallacies due to language, where Homonymy and Amphiboly (actual modes) are taken first, then Combination and Division, and Accent (potential modes), and last, Form of expression (apparent modes).[25]

Galen writes that the fact that Aristotle has the actual-potential-apparent division in mind explains the systematic order in the latter's account (104,13-14). In this passage Galen is suggesting that his own conceptual analysis (and the corresponding arguments) provides an a posteriori proof of Aristotle's insight into the nature of ambiguity and fallacy due to language.

Having paid these respects to Aristotle's wisdom, Galen shifts to the theory itself, which is Galen's own, whether or not the

---

[24] As Professor Kahn has suggested, Galen's theory may be described as a good ancient example of a 'rational reconstruction' as a technique for explaining the meaning of a philosophical text.

[25] *Soph. El.* 4. 165^{b}26-27, 165^{b}30-166^{b}19; 104,10-14.

structure of Aristotle's discussion anticipates it. Galen claims that this theory is based on the subject matter itself, that the division of ambiguity and of fallacies due to language came into being in accordance with the art of rational philosophy (the art of dialectic) as applied to reality, and hence the resulting division into six headings is a true one. Our philosopher-physician closes his discussion by comparing the art of dialectic to the art of medicine, with respect to making divisions or cuts: just as the art of medicine performs no physical cutting by chance or accidentally, so the art of dialectic makes no accidental logical cuts (104,16-17).

In *Chapter 4* Galen undertakes a selective survey of the Stoic teaching on ambiguity. Galen is interested in the Stoic doctrine not for its own sake but as a confirmation (specifically an inductive proof) that Galen's own classification is exhaustive. The proof consists in the fact that none of the kinds of ambiguity recognized by the Stoics falls outside of those specified by Galen.[26]

Galen omits any discussion of the Stoic definition of ambiguity [27] which is said to conflict with his own doctrine,[28] since it would not be to the point of the present inquiry (106,4-7). Although Galen appears to grant that the Stoics are reputable philosophers (106,4), he maintains a mocking and facetious tone toward them throughout this chapter. On the one hand, he persists in referring to the Stoics in question [29] by the overly polite 'more subtle men' (or 'more distinguished gentlemen'), and on the other, he censures them for presenting an incoherent theory (106,8; 108,11-14).

In any case, Galen turns immediately to describing and illustrating the eight kinds of ambiguity recognized by the Stoics: (1) 'Common;' (2) 'Simple Homonymy;' (3) 'Compound Homonymy;' (4) 'Ellipsis;' (5) 'Pleonasm;' (6) 'Insignificant Part Construal;' (7) 'Significant Part Construal;' and (8) 'Referability.' [30] After he expounds the Stoic teaching, Galen claims that all of their kinds of ambiguity fall under his own headings (108,12-13). And

---

[26] See 90,13-16 for Galen's characterization of an inductive proof.

[27] See *supra* p. 59.

[28] At least one way in which their definition conflicts with Galen's teaching is that it does not allow for potential ambiguity as Galen describes it at 98,17-100,2.

[29] It is reasonable to believe that these men are Chrysippus and Diogenes of Babylonia. See *infra* pp. 132-33.

[30] For a detailed description and analysis of these kinds of ambiguity, see *supra* pp. 61-68.

hence, the Stoic teaching does provide a proof that Galen's enumeration is exhaustive.

Galen then proceeds to criticize the Stoic theory, in light of his own. Galen's overall complaint is that the Stoics' doctrine lacks a scientific foundation, that it is unmethodical and unsystematic (108,13-14). Galen takes issue with their failure to adhere scrupulously to a method, a defect which deprives the kinds listed by them of any basis for being mutually exclusive [31] (108,14-15). Furthermore, Galen objects that the recognition of a kind of ambiguity called 'Compound Homonymy' is a mark of men who ignore what words mean [32]—*homonymia* derives from *homos* (same) and *onoma* (word), not from *homos* and a compound of words, i.e., a sentence.

In line with his overall complaint, Galen censures the Stoics for enumerating specific kinds of ambiguity alongside generic kinds (108,17-110,2). As an example, he cites their division of 'construed parts' to produce the specific kinds 'Insignificant Part Construal' and 'Significant Part Construal' (110,1-2). These kinds of ambiguity fall under the generic kind 'Part Construal' it would seem, and Galen is criticizing the Stoics for listing these subordinate kinds next to generic kinds, for example, 'Pleonasm.' Galen argues that by engaging in such unscientific divisions, one could extend the list of specific kinds of ambiguity greatly (110,2-3). He suggests that the so-called specific kinds of Homonymy (i.e., 'Simple Homonymy' and 'Compound Homonymy') could be increased by adding kinds on the basis of chance, analogy, and likeness (110,3-6). Clearly Galen's point is that such unmethodical dividing of generic kinds is absurd in comparison to the accurate and elegant classification of the modes of ambiguity. From Galen's point of view the Stoic theory is, in a word, incoherent, for the enumeration in which it consists is redundant and misleading.

At 110,6-7 Galen chides the Stoics for including more than one mode of ambiguity under the heading syntactic homonymy.[33] Against the Stoics Galen is presumably here urging that their

---

[31] The criticism Galen offers here clearly suggest that he considers his own modes to be mutually exclusive and that he has proved them to be so on the basis of the mutual exclusiveness of the two underlying divisions.

[32] See 108,15-17.

[33] Here Galen reverts to his own terminological framework, referring to 'modes' instead of 'kinds,' and to syntactic (ἐν λόγῳ) Homonymy.

third kind of ambiguity, 'Compound Homonymy', and their eighth kind, 'Referability,' in fact designate the same type of ambiguity (i.e., Galen's actual syntactic ambiguity, Amphiboly). Judging from the example given, we may infer that cases of 'Referability' arise from the juxtaposition of nouns in similar grammatical cases which may assume more than one grammatical role (108,9). And the example Galen provides of syntactic homonymy, 'εἴη Μέλητον Σωκράτην νικῆσαι,' ('May Socrates prevail over Meletus,' 'May Meletus prevail over Socrates') seems to meet the requirements of a case of Referability as specified above [34] (110,8-9). Hence, for Galen, Referability would seem to be one of the Stoic kinds which is improperly classified, for it is actually a subordinate kind of ambiguity which falls under, rather than beside, 'Compound Homonymy.'

Galen's final criticism of the Stoic teaching on ambiguity is that it omits reference both to apparent ambiguity and to the mode Accent (110,10-11). This is clear from the fact that no type of ambiguity that the Stoics expound, on Galen's account,[35] falls under either of his modes of Form of expression, and none is encompassed by Galen's mode Accent. In any case, the force of Galen's remark is to show that the Stoic classification is incomplete (i.e., non-exhaustive) just as he has previously suggested that its headings are not mutually exclusive.[36]

To stress the magnitude of the Stoics' oversight, Galen specifies the similarity between the mode Combination and Division (which they do recognize in their kinds 'Insignificant Part Construal' and 'Significant Part Construal') and the mode Accent. The parallels Galen draws between these kinds of ambiguity form the conclusion of *De Captionibus*. At 110,13-15 Galen states that both spoken sentences and spoken words qualify as bona fide cases of Combination and Division, and Accent. Hence, to take Galen's and Aristotle's example of Combination and Division,[37] 'Πεντήκοντ᾽

---

[34] This example is also distinctly similar in structure to that provided by Galen of Amphiboly at 88,11. It is a case of an optative of wish, followed by an infinitive (in secondary sequence), and two juxtaposed accusatives, it being unclear which is subject and which object of the infinitive.

[35] See *supra* pp. 63-64.

[36] See 108,14-15.

[37] See 88,18 and *Soph. El.* 166ª37-38. According to Galen (108,6), the Stoics give this example for their seventh kind of ambiguity, 'Significant Part Construal.'

ἀνδρῶν ἑκατὸν λίπε δῖος 'Ἀχιλλεύς,' as a spoken sentence it is a combination of words with no pauses as parts. Hence, for Galen this example as uttered is potentially ambiguous when spoken without pause—the possible variation in the placement of pause to which it is subject causes it to be ambiguous.[38] And just as pause is not a constituent part of a sentence, so accentuation is not a constituent part of a word that is a case of Accent (110,15-16). Hence, for Galen accentuation and breathings are extrinsic to a word (like 'ορος'), and when it is pronounced with indistinct pitch accent and breathing, 'ορος' is potentially ambiguous. It is the addition of spoken accentuation and breathings that causes the same word to have two distinct meanings. The Stoics omit Accent either because of its rare occurrence in speech (which is the object of their investigation), or because they apparently do not countenance a word that is indistinctly pronounced to be a word that 'strictly' has more than one meaning.

Further support for the parallel between Combination and Division, and Accent is to be found in the fact that in disputation the sophists use both pause and accentuation, and moreover, just as a man would hesitate in the presence of a case of Combination and Division when he is reading to himself, so a man under the same circumstances would hesitate over a case of Accent (110,17-112,1). Galen states that in the case of written language, it is indubitable that a person would hesitate over a sentence which is a case of Combination and Division if the dividing signs have not been added (112,1-2). Such a sentence (void of punctuation) needs the signs for the division of the words (112,2), and for the specification of the precise meaning of the sentence that is intended. In like manner, a person who confronts a case of Accent in written language, for example, 'ορος' which lacks marks of accentuation, also would hesitate. For 'ορος' needs accentuation if one is to be sure what it is intended to mean. But, Galen adds, marks of accentuation are not always needed [39] (112,3). Having spelled out the mechanics involved in disambiguating written cases of Accent, and Combination and Division, Galen abruptly ends the treatise by saying that clearly, Accent too, contrary to the Stoic doctrine, causes sentences to become ambiguous.

---

[38] See *supra* pp. 42-43.
[39] One can think of contexts in which it would be impossible for 'ορος' to be taken as anything but 'ὅρος'. In such a case, accentuation would not be required.

PART TWO

TEXT AND TRANSLATION

CHAPTER NINE

GALEN'S *DE CAPTIONIBUS*,
WITH ENGLISH TRANSLATION

The Greek *text* that follows is substantially the Gabler edition of *De Captionibus*. Additions to the text indicated by pointed brackets (< >), and deletions indicated by square brackets ([ ]) are Gabler's. The signs that appear in the apparatus criticus are:

M = Ambrosian Q3 MS.
A = Aldine editions, 1525
B = Basel edition, 1558
Ch = Charterian edition, 1639-1676
K = Kühn edition, 1821-1833
Li = H. Limanus translation, 1609
Ka = K. Kalbfleisch suggestion to Gabler
G = Gabler suggestion

In the *translation* that follows, the explanatory footnotes are those of the translator, not Galen or Gabler. Square brackets ([ ]) are employed to enclose passages added by the translator for the purpose of clarifying the line of Galen's argument, but which are not explicit in the Greek text.

ΓΑΛΗΝΟΥ

ΠΕΡΙ ΤΩΝ ΠΑΡΑ ΤΗΝ ΛΕΞΙΝ ΣΟΦΙΣΜΑΤΩΝ

Cap. I. Ἀριστοτέλης ὁ φιλόσοφος διδάσκων ἡμᾶς ἐν τῷ περὶ τῶν σοφιστικῶν ἐλέγχων συγγράμματι, παρ' ὅσους τρόπους γίγνεται τὰ παρὰ τὴν λέξιν σοφίσματα, τρόπους μὲν ἓξ τὸν ἀριθμὸν εἶναί οησιν, ἐκτίθεται δὲ αὐτοὺς οὕτως· παρ' ὁμωνυμίαν, ἀμφιβολίαν, προσῳδίαν, σύνθεσιν, διαίρεσιν, σχῆμα λέξεως. καλεῖ δὲ παρ' ὁμωνυμίαν μέν, ὅταν διὰ τῶν ὀνομάτων ἐν τῷ λόγῳ <πλείω σημαίνηται>, καθάπερ ἐν τῷ 'κύνα τεθήρακα'· πλείω γὰρ οὗτος ὁ λόγος σημαίνει διὰ τοὔνομα τὸν κύνα. παρ' ἀμφιβολίαν δέ, ὅταν παρ' αὐτὸν τὸν λόγον ἐν αὐτῷ τὸ διττὸν ᾖ καθάπερ ἔχει τὸ 'γένοιτο καταλαβεῖν τὸν ὗν ἐμέ'· ἐνταῦθα τῶν μὲν ὀνομάτων οὐδὲν διττόν, αὐτὸς δὲ ὁ λόγος ἐφ' ἑαυτοῦ σημαίνει τὸ ἑλεῖν τε καὶ ἀναιρεθῆναι. παρὰ δὲ τὴν προσῳδίαν, ὅταν <διὰ ταύτην τὸ> διττὸν γίγνηται, καθάπερ ἐν τῷ 'ὄρος ἔστηκε'· τὸ γὰρ διπλοῦν παρὰ τὴν δασεῖαν προσῳδίαν, τιθεμένην κατ' ἀρχὰς ἢ περιαιρουμένην. παρὰ δὲ τὴν σύνθεσιν καὶ διαίρεσιν, ὅταν αὕτη ποιῇ τοῦ σημαινομένου τὴν διαφοράν, ὥσπερ

Πεντήκοντ' ἀνδρῶν ἑκατὸν λίπε δῖος Ἀχιλλεύς·

---

2 περὶ τῶν κατὰ τὴν λ. σοφ. cod. Ambros. Gal. περὶ τῶν ἰδ. βιβλ. ed. K. XIX p. 47 (Scr. min. II p. 123,8 sq. Müller) 11-13 γένοιτο καταβαλεῖν τὸν ὗν ἐμέ· ἐνταῦθα γὰρ τῶν μὲν ... λόγος σφᾶς αὐτοὺς σημαίνων ἑλεῖν τε καὶ ἀναιρεθῆναι Ps.-Alex. in Soph. el. p. 138,12 sqq. Wallies. γένοιτο καταβαλεῖν ... ἐνταῦθα γὰρ τῶν μὲν ὀνομάτων οὐδὲν διττόν. ὁ δὲ λόγος idem p. 144,6 sq. γένοιτο καταβαλεῖν ... ἐμέ idem p. 27,12. γένοιτο τὸν σῦν καταβαλεῖν ἐμέ Anon. in Soph. el. p. 6,10 Hayduck. γένοιτο, Ζεῦ, τὸν σῦν καταβ. ἐμέ Alex. in Top. p. 378,3 Wallies. exemplo hic versus subest: Ὦ Ζεῦ, γένοιτο καταβαλεῖν τὸν ὗν ἐμέ Nauck² fr. adesp. 188 15-17 sqq. διὸ καὶ ὁ Γαληνὸς τοὺς παρὰ σύνθεσιν καὶ διαίρεσιν ὡς ἕνα τρόπον ἔλαβεν εἰπὼν 'παρὰ δὲ τὴν σύνθεσιν καὶ διαίρ. ... διαφοράν' Ps.-Alex. l.l. p. 142,30 sq. W.

---

3 τῶν om. BChK 5-6 φησίν, 'τίθεται M: φησὶ, τίθεται A: φησὶ, ἐκτίθεσθαι B: φησι, ἐκτίθεται ChK 6 παρωνυμίαν MA 6 ἀφιβολίαν M 7 παρωνυμίαν MA 8 πλείω σημαίνηται om. relicto sp. vac. MA: πλείω σημαίνεται in marg. add. B, in textu habet Ch 11 τὸν ὗν M: τὸ νῦν A: τὸν δ' B: τόνδ' ChK 13 διὰ ταύτην τὸ G 14 ὄρος ἔστηκε MAB δασεῖαν Ka: διττὴν M edd. 16 αὐτὴ M edd.: αὑτῇ Prantl hist. log. I p. 576: corr. Wallies 17-18 ὥσπερ πεντήκοντα ἀνδρῶν, διαιρουμένου ἀπὸ τοῦ ἑκατὸν λίπε δῖος ἀχιλλεύς post διαφοράν in marg. add. B 18 ν̄ ἀνδρῶν διαιρουμένων ἀπὸ τῶν ν̄ ἀνδρῶν ρ̄ λείπεται δεῖος ἀχιλλεύς MAB. versus exstat in Ar. org. p. 166a 37 Waitz; Ps.-Alex. p. 32,10

GALEN'S
ON FALLACIES DUE TO LANGUAGE

Chapter 1. In his treatise *On Sophistical Refutations*, the philosopher Aristotle explains to us how many modes there are in which the fallacies due to language arise.[1] He declares those modes to be six in number and lists them as follows: Homonymy, Amphiboly, Accent, Combination,[2] Division, and Form of expression. He calls a mode Homonymy when more than one thing is signified by the words in the sentence; for example, in 'I have pursued a κύων.' For this sentence signifies more than one thing because of the word 'κύων' ['dog,' 'dogstar,' 'Cynic philosopher'].

We have a case of Amphiboly when there is ambiguity in the sentence on account of the sentence as such: for example, in 'γένοιτο καταλαβεῖν τὸν ὗν ἐμέ'[3] ('May it happen that I catch the wild boar,' 'May it happen that the wild boar catch me'). There none of the words is ambiguous. The sentence as such by itself, however, signifies both the catching and the being caught by [the wild boar].

We have a case of Accent when ambiguity arises because of the accent; for example, in 'ορος stands' ('a hill (ὄρος) stands,' 'a boundary (ὅρος) stands'). For the ambiguity occurs on account of the aspirated accent, which is either placed at the beginning or omitted.

We have a case of Combination and Division when it is this which makes the difference in what is meant,[4] as in 'Πεντήκοντ' ἀνδρῶν ἑκατὸν λίπε δῖος Ἀχιλλεύς,' ('Noble Achilles left fifty of a hundred men,' 'Noble Achilles left a hundred of fifty men').[5]

---

[1] I have rendered 'λέξις' throughout by 'language,' except in the name of the mode σχῆμα τῆς λέξεως which is translated as 'Form of expression.' This follows the Oxford canon. The term 'λέξις' literally means 'speech,' 'diction,' 'style,' or 'vocabulary' and can refer to the letter of the text as contrasted with its meaning.

[2] 'Composition' is the classical rendering of 'σύνθεσις,' but I follow the Oxford and Loeb translations of the *Sophistici Elenchi* which use 'Combination.'

[3] See *infra* p. 117-18.

[4] 'σημαίνω' is rendered indifferently 'signify' or 'mean.'

[5] Admittedly the second rendering is arithmetically impossible. The sentence may also be taken as 'Noble Achilles left 150 of the men.' On this example of Combination and Division see *infra* pp. 119-20.

ἡ γὰρ διαφορὰ τοῦ ἀνδρῶν ἢ <συντιθεμένου ἢ> διαιρουμένου ἀπὸ τῶν ν' ἐστι. παρὰ δὲ τὸ σχῆμα τῆς λέξεως, ὁπόταν ἕτερον τῷ ὄντι σημαίνῃ, ἕτερον δὲ διὰ τὸ εἶδος καὶ τὸ σχῆμα δοκῇ [δέ], οἷον τὸ 'ἀκούω' ἔστι μὲν τοῦ πάσχειν, δόξειε δ' ἂν τοῦ ποιεῖν διὰ τὴν προφοράν, ὅπερ ἐστὶ τὸ
5 σχῆμα † παραπλήσια κρατεῖσθαι τοῖς τοῦ ποιεῖν, τῷ τρέχω καὶ νοῶ· ἑλκύσει γὰρ ἂν ὁ σοφιστικὸς πρὸς ἑκάτερον· πρὸς μὲν τὸ πάσχειν, ὅτι ἔστι, πρὸς δὲ τὸ ποιεῖν, ὅτι φαίνεται. τούτους δ' ἐξηριθμημένος τοὺς τρόπους ἐφεξῆς δείκνυσιν, ὅτι [τὸ] μηδεὶς ἔστιν, ὃν παραλέλοιπε, μηδὲ οἷόν τέ ἐστι τῶν παρὰ τὴν λέξιν τι σοφισμάτων ἔξω πεσεῖν τῶν εἰρημένων.
10 ὁ δὲ λόγος, δι' οὗ ταῦτα δείκνυσιν, ἐστὶν οὗτος· 'τούτου δὲ πίστις ἡ διὰ τῆς ἐπαγωγῆς καὶ συλλογισμός, ἄν τε ληφθῇ τις ἕτερος, καὶ ὅ τι τοσαυταχῶς ἂν τοῖς αὐτοῖς ὀνόμασι καὶ λόγοις μὴ ταὐτὸν [μέντοι] δηλώσαιμεν'. τὸ μὲν οὖν τῆς ἐπαγωγῆς γνώριμον· εἰ γὰρ καθ' ἕκαστον εἰπόντι καὶ λαβόντι τῶν παρὰ τὴν λέξιν σοφισμάτων
15 φαίνοιτο μηδὲν πίπτειν ἔξω τῶν εἰρημένων τρόπων, δῆλον ἤδη ταύτῃ γε, ὅτι μηδεὶς παραλέλειπται τρόπος· τὸ δ' ἐφεξῆς παντάπασιν ἀσαφές ἐστι, τί ποτε βούλεται λέγειν ἐν τῷ 'καὶ συλλογισμός, ἄν τε ληφθῇ τις ἕτερος, <καὶ ὅτι τοσαυταχῶς ἂν> τοῖς αὐτοῖς ὀνόμασι καὶ λόγοις οὐ ταὐτὰ δηλώσαιμεν'· οὐδὲ γὰρ ὅπως ἂν ἕτερόν
20 τινα λάβοιμεν συλλογισμὸν εἴρηται, τὸ δὲ 'καὶ ὅτι τοσαυταχῶς ἂν τοῖς αὐτοῖς ὀνόμασι καὶ λόγοις οὐ ταὐτὰ δηλώσαιμεν' συλλογισμοῦ συμπεράσματι μᾶλλον ἔοικεν ἢ συλλογισμῷ. σύνηθες δὲ τὸ τοιοῦτον τάχος τῷ φιλοσόφῳ καὶ καθάπερ ἐπὶ σημείων ἐκφέρειν τὰ

---

1 τοῦ] τῶν MAB: corr. Ch   τοῦ post ἀνδρῶν add. ChK   συντιθεμένου ἢ (composito cum quinquaginta aut) add. LiChK   2 σημαίνει MABCh:. corr. K   3 δοκῇ [δέ] (significare videtur) Li: δοκεῖ δὲ M edd.   4 δόξειε δ' Ka: δόξης (δόξῃς) M edd.   5 παραπλήσιον ChK: possis sic corrigere σχῆμα· παραπλησία γάρ ἐστι: Ka ita velit διὰ <τὸ, cf. v. 8> τὴν προφοράν, ὅπερ ἐ. τ. σχ., παραπλησίαν κεκτῆσθαι   τῷ G: τοῦ M edd.   7 ἐξαριθμημένους MAB: ἐξηριθμημένους ChK: corr. Ka   8 τὸ M: eiecit A   ὃν MAB   9 μὲν post παρὰ add. ChK   10 ἡ M: ἥ τε edd. ex Arist. l.l. p. 165b 27   11 ἕτερος] ἄλλος Arist.   13 ταὐτὰ Waitzii codd. Tui, cf. v. 21   [μέντοι] G: cf. v. 19; v. 21; p. 102,20   15 μήτ' ἐμπίπτειν MAB: corr. Ch   16 ἐφ' ἑξῆς MABCh   17 συλλογισμὸν MAB: corr. Ch   18 καὶ ὅτι τοσαυταχῶς ἂν (et quod tot modis) add. LiChK, om. spatiolo rel. MA, stellula interp. B   19 γὰρ Ka: γε M edd.   20 ἂν erasum esse videtur in M   22 συμπέρασμά τι M

For the difference depends upon whether 'men' [is considered] combined with or separated from 'fifty'.[6]

We have a case of Form of expression when one thing is really signified, but by virtue of the form and figure,[7] something else appears to be meant. For example, 'ἀκούω'[8] ('I hear') is a verb of passivity; however, it would appear to be a verb of activity on account of the outward expression, that is, its form.[9] For the form is similar to verbs of activity, like 'τρέχω' ('I run') and 'νοῶ' ('I think'). Now the sophistical argument will twist it both ways— will take it as a passivity because it is a passivity, but also as activity, since it appears to be an activity [by virtue of its form].

Having enumerated these modes, Aristotle next shows that no mode has been omitted and that it is not possible that any fallacy due to language falls outside those mentioned. And the argument by which he shows this is as follows: 'To show this, there is a proof by induction and a syllogism, (and perhaps there is some other [syllogism] that may be taken), that this is the number of ways in which we may fail to mean the same thing by the same words and sentences.'[10]

Now the inductive procedure is familiar. For if when a man states and accepts the fallacies due to language one by one, none is observed to fall outside the modes mentioned, then it is obvious at least in this way [i.e. inductively] that no mode has been omitted. But what Aristotle says next is wholly unclear; namely, what he means by 'and a syllogism, (and perhaps there is some other [syllogism] that may be taken), that this is the number of ways in which we may fail to mean the same things by the same words and sentences.' For it has not been stated how we could take some other syllogism, and the sentence, 'this is the number of ways in which we may fail to mean the same things by the same words and sentences,' resembles a syllogistic conclusion more than a syllogism.

But it is customary for the Philosopher to speak with such brevity and to express many of his points as it were by signals,

---

[6] This translation depends on a textual emendation. See *infra* p. 120.

[7] Here 'form' is the rendering of 'εἶδος' and 'figure' is that of 'σχῆμα.'

[8] Grammatically speaking, 'ἀκούω' is a (first person, present indicative) active verb.

[9] Here 'σχῆμα' is rendered 'form.' The translation of this passage is based on an emendation of the Gabler text. See *infra* pp. 120-21.

[10] *Soph. El.* 4. 165ᵇ27-30.

πολλὰ [καὶ] διὰ τὸ πρὸς τοὺς ἀκηκοότας ἤδη γράφεσθαι. τῶν οὖν ἐξηγησαμένων αὐτὸν οἱ μὲν οὐδ' ἐπεχείρησαν ταῦτ' ἀκριβῶσαι τὸν προσήκοντα τρόπον, οἱ δ' οὐκ ἔτυχον. ἡμεῖς δὲ πειραθῶμεν, οὐκ Ἀριστοτέλους ἕνεκεν οὐδ' ὡς τῷ λόγῳ βοήθειάν τινα πορίζοντες, ἀλλ' ἡμῶν αὐτῶν·
5 φιλοσόφου γὰρ οὐ μόνον τὰς προτάσεις λαβόντα συλλογίσασθαι, καθάπερ τοῖς πλείστοις <ἔθος>, ἀλλὰ καὶ τοῦ συμπεράσματος κειμένου τὰς προτάσεις κατασκευάσαι.

Cap. II. Ἐπεὶ δὲ δεῖξαι πρόκειται τοσαυταχῶς γίγνεσθαι τὰ παρὰ τὴν λέξιν σοφίσματα, ὁσαχῶς Ἀριστοτέλης ἔφη τὰ παρὰ τὸ διττόν,
10 δῆλον ὡς δύο δεικτέον ἡμῖν, ἓν μὲν ὅτι πάντα τὰ παρὰ τὴν λέξιν παρὰ τὸ διττόν ἐστιν, ἕτερον δ' ὅτι παρὰ τὸ διττὸν τοσαῦτα. δῆλον δ' ἐκεῖνό γε πᾶσιν, ὅτι πάντα τὰ παρὰ τὴν λέξιν σοφίσματα παρὰ κακίαν αὐτῆς ἀνάγκη συμβαίνειν· ταύτης γὰρ ὥσπερ ἀρχῆς ἐχόμενοι καὶ ἐξαπατῶσιν οἱ σοφισταὶ τοὺς ἀπειροτέρους ἐν τούτοις καὶ μὴ συνορῶντας τὸ κίβδηλον.
15 εἰ δὴ βουλοίμεθα καλῶς λαβεῖν, ὁπόσα παρὰ τὴν λέξιν συμβαίνει σοφίσματα, ληπτέον, πόσαι ποτ' εἰσὶν <αὐτῆς αἱ κακίαι>· ὃ ἂν συνοφθείη τῆς ἀρετῆς ληφθείσης εἴτε ἐστὶ μία εἴτε πλείους· [ἀπασῶν] ἁμαρτία γὰρ τῆς ἀρετῆς ἔοικεν εἶναι <κακία> καὶ ταύτης ὀρθῶς ληφθείσης εὐθὺς κἀκείνη γνωρίζεσθαι. ἐπεὶ δέ, καθάπερ <ἐν> ἑτέροις ἀποδέδεικται λόγοις,
20 τὸ εὖ τε καὶ ἡ ἀρετὴ ἐν ἐκείνῳ, πρὸς ὃ πέφυκεν ἢ γέγονεν, ἀνθρώπου μὲν τὸ ζῆν, μαχαίρας δὲ τὸ τέμνειν, ληπτέον ἂν εἴη τὸ πρὸς τί πέφυκεν ἢ γέγονεν ἡ λέξις. φαίνεται δὲ πρὸς ἕν, τὸ σημαίνειν· δῆλον οὖν ὅτι καὶ

---

1 [καὶ] G   6 ἔθος G: εἴωθεν add. ChK   9 τὰ παρὰ τὸ διττὸν cf. p. 90, 12 et p. 98,1   13 καὶ om. ChK   14 συνορῶντες MA: corr. B   16 αὐτῆς αἱ κακίαι G (vitia Li): αἱ κακίαι ἐν αὐτῇ ChK, quod non recepi propter hiatum 17 (post ληφθείσης) εἴτε] εἴπερ M edd.   [ἀπασῶν] G   18 κακία add. Ka   κἀκείνη G: κἀκείνην M edd.   19 ἐν add. ChK   21 μὲν <ἐν> τῷ et δ' ἐν τῷ coni. Ka   πρὸς τό τι MAB: corr. Ch

since he is writing for those who have already heard [his explanation]. Hence, some of his commentators did not even try to give a precise and appropriate explanation of this passage, and others just did not succeed. But let us make the attempt, not for Aristotle's sake, nor in order to come to the defense of the passage, but for our own sake. For it is a mark of a philosopher not only to accept premises and draw a conclusion, as most do, but also to construct the premises of a given conclusion.

Chapter 2. Since our task is to show that the fallacies due to language arise in the same number of ways Aristotle said fallacies due to ambiguity arise, it is clear we must show two things—first, that all the fallacies due to language are fallacies due to ambiguity; and second, that the fallacies due to ambiguity are just as many [in number as Aristotle said].

Now this at least is plain to everyone, that all the fallacies due to language necessarily result from vice of language. For it is by holding fast to this [namely, to vice in language] as to a first principle that the sophists deceive those who are less experienced in these matters and who do not perceive the fraud.

If we wish to determine accurately how many fallacies result from language, we must determine how many vices in language there are. This will be fully seen when it has been determined whether the virtue of language is one or more than one. For vice seems to be a failure of [the corresponding] virtue, and as soon as the latter is correctly determined, the former immediately can also be recognized. And since, as has been proved in other discussions, the excellence and the virtue [of anything] are in that for which the thing is suited by nature or for which it has come into being—for a man, living, and for a blade, cutting—we should determine that for which language is suited by nature or for which it has come into being [11] [i.e., its function]. And it seems that it has one function, signifying.[12] Consequently, it is clear

---

[11] This awkward phrase specifies a natural or artificial thing's *function* and I henceforth render the corresponding Greek by 'function.' Galen refrains from using the terms 'τέλος' ('end') and 'ἔργον' ('function'), however, in his treatise.

[12] 'σημαίνειν' ('signifying') is a key term in Galen's whole theory. It means signifying or indicating *meaning*, that is, communicating thought or information. Literally the verb means 'to give sign,' from 'σῆμα,' a sign, signal, or marker, for example, a road sign. See Aristotle's *Rhet.* 3. 2. 1404ᵇ1-5, where the idea is rendered by 'δηλοῦν.'

<τὸ> εὖ καὶ κακῶς ἐν τούτῳ. δῆλον δὲ ὅτι καὶ μόνη τῶν ἀρετῶν αὕτη κατ' αὐτὴν τὴν λέξιν, αἱ δ' ἄλλαι κατὰ συμβεβηκὸς καὶ ἔξωθεν καὶ οὐ τοῦ πράγματος, οἷον εὐαρμοστία καὶ εὐγραμματία· τοῦτο γὰρ εἰ καὶ φαίνεταί τισιν εὖ, ἀλλ' οὐ κατὰ τὸ πρᾶγμα, ἀλλ' ὥσπερ εἰ ξίφος ἐλεφαντόκωπον
5 εἴη ἢ ὀφθαλμὸς ὑπογεγραμμένος· καὶ γὰρ τούτοις ταῦτα ἔξωθεν. τὰ δὲ κατ' αὐτὰ ἐν τῷ τέμνειν τε καὶ ὁρᾶν. εἰ δὴ ταύτην ἀρετὴν ἑκάστου τυγχάνειν ὀρθῶς λέγεται, καθ' ἣν ἕδραν ἔχει, πρὸς ὃ πέφυκεν ἢ γέγονεν, δῆλον ὡς καὶ τὸν ἀριθμὸν τῶν ἀρετῶν ἐντεῦθεν ἄν τις <λάβοι> ὁπόσος ἐστίν· εἰ μὲν γὰρ πρὸς πολλά, πλείους, εἰ δὲ πρὸς ἕν, μία. φαίνεταί γε μὴν
10 ἡ λέξις πρὸς ἕν, τὸ σημαίνειν· εἴπερ <οὖν> τὸ καλῶς πρὸς τοῦτο <ἀνήκει, κακία τῆς λέξεως, ἔσται τὸ> μὴ σημαίνειν ἢ μὴ εὖ σημαίνειν. καίτοι ἴσως δεῖται σκέψεως εἰ θετέον εἶναι λέξιν ἔτι τὴν μὴ σημαίνουσαν· οὐδὲ γὰρ αὐλητὴς ὁ μὴ πεφυκὼς αὐλεῖν ὅλως· οὐκοῦν οὐδὲ κακὸς αὐλητής· οὐδὲ λέξεως ἄρα κακία τὸ μὴ σημαίνειν· τοῦτο δὲ εὐθὺς καὶ σημεῖον τοῦ
15 μόνην τὴν ὑφ' ἡμῶν [τούτων δὲ] λεγομένην ἀρετὴν εἶναι τῆς λέξεως καθ' αὑτήν· ἐν ᾧ γὰρ ἑκάστῳ τὸ εἶναι, ἐν τούτῳ καὶ ἡ ἀρετή· ἡ δὲ λέξις ἐν τῷ σημαίνειν, τούτου γέ τοι διαφθαρέντος οὐδὲ λέξις· οὐκοῦν ἐν τούτῳ καὶ ἡ ἀρετή. διὸ καὶ μόνη συναποβάλλεται, αἱ δ' ἄλλαι διὰ τὸ μὴ κατ' αὐτὸ τὸ πρᾶγμα εἶναι οὐδὲν κωλύονται καὶ περὶ τὴν μὴ σημαίνουσαν
20 ὑπάρχειν, οἷον ἡ εὐαρμοστία καὶ ἡ εὐγραμματία. κρείττω γοῦν διὰ ταῦτα

---

1 τὸ add. Ka   2 καθ' αὐτὴν τῆς λέξεως ChK   4 ἐλεφαντάκοπον MAB: corr. Ch   6 καθ' αὐτὰ MChK   εἰ δὴ (si igitur) Li: ἤδη MAB   7 ὀρθῶς Ka: εἴθ' ὡς M edd.   ἔχειν M edd.: corr. Ka   8 λάβοι G: γνοίη add. ChK   10 οὖν G   11 ἀνήκει ... τὸ G   κακία ἔσται post σημαίνειν add. ChK (vitium erit Li)   13 οὐκοῦν M   15 ὑφ' ὑμῶν per compendium scriptum M: ὑφ' ἡμᾶς AB: corr. Ch   [τούτων δὲ] G: τούτων om. ChK   λεγομένων ἀρετὴ MAB: corr. Ch   16 ἑκάστου ChK   τὸ εἰσὶν MA: corr. B   17 γέ] γὰρ? Ka   οὔκουν M   20 ὑπάρξιν MAB: corr. Ch

that both its excellence and its poor quality are found in this [namely, in signifying].

Furthermore, it is also plain that among the virtues [of language] this alone[13] is the virtue of language per se, whereas the other virtues [of language] are accidental, external, and not essential to the thing [i.e., language]; for example, sonority and calligraphy. For even if to some men these appear excellent, nevertheless, they are not essential to the thing, but it is as if a sword had an ivory hilt or an eye had eye shadow applied to it. For these excellences are external to the sword or the eye; their per se excellences lie in their cutting and seeing.

If now it is truly said that this is the virtue of each thing, in accordance with which the thing has its place [in the world], this,[14] namely the thing's function, then it is clearly on that basis that one would determine how many [essential] virtues the thing has. For if a thing has many functions, then it has several virtues, but if it has one function, then it has one virtue.

Now surely it seems that language has one function; namely, signifying. But if its excellence attaches to this, the vice of language will be either not signifying or not signifying well. However, we should perhaps consider whether language which does not signify [at all] should still be admitted as language. For the man not naturally endowed for flute-playing at all is not a flutist; therefore, he is not a bad flutist. Consequently, not signifying is not a vice of language.

Now this [to wit: that we do not admit as language that which does not signify] is precisely a sign that only the virtue we mentioned [15] is a virtue of language per se. For in each case, the virtue of a thing and its essence are found in the same principle. [The essence of] language is in signifying; and when this has been destroyed, there is no language either. Therefore, its virtue also lies in signifying. For this reason, [the essential virtue of language] alone is lost at the same time [as the signifying], whereas the other virtues, being nonessential to the thing, may still belong to language that does not signify; for example, sonority and calligraphy.

---

[13] This virtue of language per se is excellence in signifying, or 'signifying well.'

[14] The translation of this sentence is based on a textual emendation. See *infra* p. 125.

[15] This virtue is signifying well, mentioned at 94,1 and 94,11.

καὶ τῶν βαρβαρικῶν διαλέκτων ἑτέραν ἑτέρας φαμέν, οἷον τὴν Περσίδα τῆς Αἰθιοπικῆς, καίτοι μὴ σημαίνουσαν ἡμῖν· τὸ δ' αἴτιον, ὅτι φωνῆς μᾶλλον <ποιοῦμεν κρ>ίσιν ἢ λέξεως· ἀλλ' εἴ τῳ καὶ δοκεῖ τοῦτο κακία, τὸ μὴ σημαίνειν, καὶ πλανᾶταί τις <τῷ> διὰ τὴν ὁμοιότητα <κακίαν>
5 καὶ τοῦ <το> καλεῖσθαι, ἀλλ' ἐκεῖνό γε δῆλον, ὡς οὐδὲν ἂν διὰ ταύτην <τὴν> κακίαν σόφισμα συμβαίη· τίς γὰρ ἂν ὁμολογήσειεν ἢ θείη τι πρὸς ἄσημον καὶ ἀσαφῆ λέξιν; λείπεται δὴ διὰ τὸ <μὴ> εὖ σημαίνειν· τοῦτο δὲ ὅτι διττῶς· ἐν τούτῳ γὰρ ὑπάρχει μόνῳ τῇ λέξει σημαίνειν μέν τι, μὴ εὖ δὲ σημαίνειν· τὸ γὰρ 'κύων' ὄνομα σημαίνει μέν τι, οὕτω δὲ
10 τόδε τι οὐδὲ ἀφωρισμένον, ὅπερ ἦν τὸ εὔληπτον. κἀκεῖνο δὲ λέγεται καλῶς ὑπὸ Πλάτωνος, ὅτι πάντα, ὅσα φθαρτά, τῇ σφετέρᾳ κακίᾳ φθείρεται· φθείρει δὲ καὶ τοῦτο τὴν λέξιν· ἄγει γὰρ ἀπειρότερόν τινα εἰς ἀσάφειαν, ἀλλ' οὐχὶ ἁπλῶς, ὥσπερ τὰ μηδὲν σημαίνοντα· ἡ δ' ἀσάφεια καὶ πρόσθεν ἐλέγετο διαφθορά τις εἶναι παντελὴς τῆς λέξεως· ὥστε πάλιν καὶ
15 διὰ τοῦτο μόνη κακία τὸ διττόν, χωρὶς εἰ μή τις οἴεται κἀκεῖνα κακίας οἷον ἔνδειαν ἢ μακρολογίαν ἢ περιττολογίαν· λανθάνει δὲ τοῦτο, νομίζω, ἀπατώμενος καὶ μὴ συνιείς, ὅτι τούτων οὐδὲν ἁπλῶς κακὸν τῆς λέξεως, εἰ μὴ τὴν ἀσάφειαν ἢ τὸ διττὸν ἐργάζοιτο. εἰ δὲ μόνη κακία λέξεως αὕτη καὶ καλῶς τὰ πρόσθεν εἴρηται, πάντα δὲ τὰ παρὰ τὴν λέξιν σοφίσματα
20 παρὰ τὴν κακίαν ταύτην γίγνεται, πάντα τὰ παρὰ τὴν λέξιν ἔσται παρὰ τὸ διττόν.

11 σχεδὸν πᾶσι ξύμφυτον ἑκάστῳ κακόν τε καὶ νόσημα ... Plato Reipubl. X c. 9 p. 609 A. ὥσπερ σῶμα ἢ σώματος πονηρία νόσος οὖσα τήκει καὶ διόλλυσι καὶ ἄγει εἰς τὸ μηδὲ σῶμα εἶναι, καὶ ἃ νῦν δὴ ἐλέγομεν ἅπαντα ὑπὸ τῆς οἰκείας κακίας, τῷ προσκαθῆσθαι καὶ ἐνεῖναι διαφθειρούσης. εἰς τὸ μὴ εἶναι ἀφικνεῖται — οὐχ οὕτως; Ναί. Ἴθι δή. καὶ ψυχὴν κατὰ τὸν αὐτὸν τρόπον σκόπει et sqq. l.l. p. 609 C.

3 ποιοῦμεν κρίσιν G: ἴσην MAB: φωνὴ μᾶλλόν ἐστιν ἢ λέξις ChK   κακία] κἀκεῖνα MB: κακεῖνα A: corr. Li (vitium)   4 τῷ, κακίαν, -το suppl. Ka   5 γε Ka: δὲ M edd.   οὐδ' ἐναντία MAB: οὐδ' ἂν διὰ ChK: corr. Ka   6 τὴν add. Ka   συνθείη ChK   τι Ka: τὶς (τίς) M edd.   7 ἀσαφῆ (ignotam) LiChK: σαφῆ MAB   μὴ (non) add. LiChK   8 διττόν ChK   μόνη MAB: μόνῃ ChK: corr. Ka   9 μέντοι M: corr. A   10 τὸ δέ τι MABCh (hoc aliquid Li)   ἀφωρισμένος M: corr. A   δὲ κἀκεῖνο MAB: corr. Ch
11-12 φθείρεται. φθείρεται δὲ καὶ του' M: φθείρεται δὲ καὶ τούτων AB: φθείρει δὲ καὶ τούτων ChK (corrumpit Li)   12 πρότερον M edd.: corr. Ka; cf. p. 92,14   12-13 ἀσαφείαν MAB   13 ἀσαφεία MAB   14 πρόσθεν] p. 94,17   ὥσπερ πᾶν M edd.: corr. Ka   15 τι MAB: corr. Ch   18 ἢ] εἰ MAB: corr. Li (aut)   19 τὰ παρὰ τὰ σοφίσματα MAB: corr. Ch   20 αὐτὴν MAB: corr. Ch

Thus, on the basis of these factors at least, we say that one foreign language [16] is superior to another—for example that Persian is superior to Ethiopian—even though it does not signify anything for us. And the reason is that we make a judgment of sound rather than of language.

But if someone thinks this is a vice [of language], namely, the failure to signify [or be meaningful], and if he is misled by the fact that because of a resemblance [between 'not signifying' and 'not signifying well'] this also is called a vice, still it is at any rate clear that no fallacy could occur because of this vice [i.e., not signifying]. For who would accept or propose a premise on the basis of language that is insignificant and obscure? We are left with the alternative [that fallacy can result] from language not signifying well. And this [i.e., signifying poorly] occurs because it signifies ambiguously. For in this way alone can language signify something, but not signify [it] well. For the word 'κύων' [17] signifies something, but not yet something definite or distinct, which is what we mean by something easy to grasp.

Plato put this well [when he said] that all things that are corruptible, are corrupted by their own vice. And ambiguity corrupts language. For it leads a less experienced man into obscurity, but not unqualified obscurity, as in the case of that which signifies nothing. But we have already said that obscurity [in that sense] is a complete destruction of language. So let this be one more reason for the claim that ambiguity is the only vice, unless someone thinks that there are other vices, such as elliptical utterance, prolixity, or redundance. But I believe the man who claims this is deceived, and does not understand, unaware as he is, that none of these is without qualification a vice of language, unless it produces obscurity or ambiguity.

If this is the sole vice of language and our earlier statements are correct, and if all the fallacies due to language arise because of this vice, then all the fallacies due to language will be fallacies due to ambiguity.

---

[16] This is the sole place in this treatise where the word rendered 'language' is not 'λέξις,' but 'διάλεκτος.'

[17] 'κύων' may be rendered 'dog,' 'dogstar,' and 'Cynic philosopher.' It occurs earlier at 88,9 as an example of a homonym.

ΠΕΡΙ ΤΩΝ ΠΑΡΑ ΤΗΝ ΛΕΞΙΝ ΣΟΦΙΣΜΑΤΩΝ

Cap. III. Δεικτέον δὲ τὸ μετὰ τοῦτ' ἂν εἴη, διὰ τί τὰ παρὰ τὸ διττὸν τοσαυταχῶς, ὁσαχῶς Ἀριστοτέλης φησί, συνίσταται. εἰ δὲ καὶ τοῦτο μέλλει καλῶς εὑρεθήσεσθαι, ληπτέον πρότερον, ὅ, τι ποτέ ἐστι λόγος τε καὶ † ἐκ λόγων. λόγοι γὰρ καὶ αἱ προτάσεις· τούτων <δ' ἓν> τινὶ ἢ
5 τισὶ διττόν <τι> ζητοῦμεν. ἔσται δὴ λόγος, ὡς πρὸς τὸ παρὸν ἀποχρώντως εἰπεῖν, σύνθεσις ὀνομάτων· καλῶ δὲ ὀνόματα νῦν καὶ τὰ ῥήματα καὶ ὅλως ὅ, τι σημαίνει, διὰ τὸ γνωριμώτερον. ἀνάγκη <δὴ> τὸ διττὸν ἢ ἕν τινι τούτων εἶναι τῶν ὀνομάτων ἢ ἐν αὐτῷ τῷ λόγῳ· τρίτον γὰρ οὐδὲν ἔχομεν ὅπως συσταίη ποτ' ἄν, ὥσπερ οὐδ' ἄν τις ἔχοι *** παρ'
10 ἕκαστα τῶν λίθων ἢ τὸ συγκείμενον. καὶ τοῦτο ἢ ἐνεργείᾳ ἢ δυνάμει ἢ φαντασίᾳ· παρὰ ταῦτα γὰρ οὐδὲν <ἂν> ἕτερόν τις εὕροι ὑπάρχον ἢ λεγόμενον, καθάπερ ἐν ἄλλοις ἀποδέδεικται. πάντα δὲ ταῦτα συλλαβόντες ἔχουσιν οἱ εἰρημένοι τρόποι· ἐνεργείᾳ μὲν γὰρ τὸ διττὸν ἔχουσι παρά τε τὴν ὁμωνυμίαν καὶ τὴν ἀμφιβολίαν, καὶ <ἐν> ὀνόματι μὲν ὁ παρὰ τὴν
15 ὁμωνυμίαν, ἐν λόγῳ δὲ ὁ παρὰ τὴν ἀμφιβολίαν, ἐνεργείᾳ δέ, ὅτι τῷ ὄντι δύο σημαίνουσι· δυνάμει δ' ὁπότε τῇ προσῳδίᾳ γίγνονται διττοί, καὶ παρὰ τὴν σύνθεσιν καὶ διαίρεσιν· οὗτοι γὰρ οὐ σημαίνουσι πλείω,

---

5-6 ἐπεὶ γὰρ ὁ λόγος σύνθεσίς ἐστιν ὀνομάτων (ῥητέον δὲ καὶ νῦν, ὡς πολλάκις εἴπομεν. ὀνόματα καὶ τὰ ῥήματα), τὸ διττὸν ἢ ἕν τισι τούτων τῶν ὀνομάτων ἐστὶν ἢ ἐν αὐτῷ τῷ λόγῳ. Ps.-Alex. l.l. p. 28,8 sqq.   9 sqq. ἐνεργείᾳ μὲν οὖν τὸ διττὸν ἔχουσιν οἱ παρὰ τὴν ὁμωνυμίαν καὶ τὴν ἀμφιβολίαν σοφισμοί, ἐν ὀνόματι μὲν οἱ παρὰ τὴν ὁμωνυμίαν, ἐν λόγῳ δὲ οἱ παρὰ τὴν ἀμφιβολίαν· ἐνεργείᾳ δέ, ὅτι τῷ ὄντι δύο σημαίνουσι. Ps.-Alex. l.l. p. 22,36 sqq. ἐνεργείᾳ μὲν οὖν ἔχοιεν τὸ διττὸν οἱ παρὰ τὴν ὁμωνυμίαν καὶ ἀμφιβολίαν Anon. in Soph. el. p. 10,4 sq. Hayduck.   16 δυνάμει δὲ τὸ διττὸν ἔχουσι οἱ παρὰ τὴν προσῳδίαν καὶ τὴν σύνθεσιν καὶ τὴν διαίρεσιν· οὗτοι γὰρ πλείω μὲν οὐ σημαίνουσιν, ἀλλὰ πάντως ἕν· διὰ δὲ τὸ ἑκατέρως δέχεσθαι διττοὶ λέγονται. διὸ καὶ δυνάμει φαμὲν αὐτούς, τοιοῦτον γὰρ τὸ δυνάμει. Ps.-Alex. l.l. p. 23,4 sqq.   δυνάμει δὲ οἱ παρὰ προσῳδίαν καὶ σύνθεσιν καὶ διαίρεσιν· πλείω μὲν γὰρ οὐ σημαίνουσι, διὰ δὲ τὸ εἰς ἑκάτερον ἐκλαμβάνεσθαι διττοὶ λέγονται. Anon. in Soph. el. p. 10,7 sqq.

1 τά] τὸ M edd.: corr. Ka   2 ὅσα χωρὶς MAB: corr. Li (quot modis) τλ ἡ
ἄφιστο φ M   4 possis scribere ἐκ τίνων s. ἐκ <τίνων> λόγοι   δ' ἓν G
5 τι G   6 σύνθεσιν M: corr. A   7 ὅ, τι G: τι M edd.   γνωριμώτερα M edd.   δὴ add. Ka   9 συσταίη, ὁπόταν M edd.: corr. Ka   ἄν τις ἔχοι] ἀντέχει MAB: corr. Ch   9-10 ἔχοι κατ' οἰκίαν κακὸν οὐδὲν ἐνδείκνυσθαι παρ' ἕκαστον proponit Ka   10 τούτῳ MAB: corr. Ch   11 ἂν add. Ka   12 ἐν ἄλλοις] fort. in commentariis quibus Eudemi Περὶ λέξεως libros explicavit (cf. p. 102,16 et De libris suis 14 p. 123,5 M)   13 τε] τὸ MA: corr. B   14 ἐν add. ChK   15 ὁμωνυμίαν MA   16 γιγνόμενοι MAB: corr. Li (fiunt)   17 οὐ (non) Li: ὅτε MAB

Chapter 3. The next step is to show why the fallacies due to ambiguity are produced in as many ways as Aristotle says they are. And if this is to be successfully investigated, we must first determine what a sentence is and of what a sentence consists.[18] For the premises [of arguments] are sentences. [And when we are inquiring into fallacy,] we are inquiring into ambiguity in one or more sentences. For our present purposes, it will suffice to define a sentence as a combination of names.[19] And among names I am now including verbs, and in general, whatever signifies something, since this is a more familiar way [of speaking; that is, to use the term 'name' to mean word in general].[20]

It is necessary that ambiguity be situated either in some one of the words or in the sentence as such [i.e., in the combination of words]. For we have no third way in which it might be produced, just as in the case of a house, there would be nothing one could find fault with except the stones taken severally or the composite of them.[21] Now ambiguity is actual, potential, or apparent. For these are the only ways of existing or of being spoken of, as has been proved elsewhere.[22]

And the stated modes [giving rise to the fallacies due to language] have all these properties pairwise.[23] For cases of Homonymy and Amphiboly have actual ambiguity; Homonymy having lexical[24] ambiguity and Amphiboly having syntactic[25] ambiguity; and the ambiguity is actual since [cases of] Homonymy and Amphiboly do in fact signify two things.

The ambiguity is potential when it arises from Accent, and from Combination and Division. For [cases of] these modes do

---

[18] Gabler here marks the text as corrupt. The translation is based on one of Gabler's suggestions in the apparatus. See *infra* p. 127.

[19] Literally, a sentence is said to be a 'putting together of names,' a 'σύνθεσις ὀνομάτων.'

[20] Henceforth, 'ὄνομα' is rendered 'word' instead of 'name' in keeping with the broad usage to which Galen here subscribes.

[21] There is a gap here in the text. I translate a suggestion of Kalbfleisch that is included in the apparatus. See *infra* p. 128.

[22] That is, elsewhere it has been shown that for any entity, it exists actually, potentially, or apparently, and it may be spoken of as being actual, potential, or apparent.

[23] Each mode has one property from each of the two sets of properties as a basis for its classification and as a basis for its definition.

[24] Literally, 'ἐν ὀνόματι' means 'in a word.'

[25] Literally, 'ἐν λόγῳ' means 'in a sentence.'

ἀλλὰ πάντως ἕν, διὰ δὲ τὸ ἑκάτερον ἐνδέχεσθαι διττοὶ λέγονται· δ.ὸ καὶ δυνάμει φαμὲν αὐτούς. τοιοῦτον γὰρ τὸ δυνάμει. [οἷον] τοῦτο <δ'> αὖ πάλιν, ὥσπερ καὶ πρόσθεν διῄρητο, ἢ ἐν ὀνόμασιν ἢ ἐν λόγῳ. ἐν μὲν οὖν ὀνόμασιν ἡ προσῳδία ποιεῖ τὸ διττόν· αὕτη γὰρ ἐφ' ἑκάτερον ἕλκει
5 τοὔνομα, ὥσπερ ἐν τῷ 'ορος ἕστηκεν' ἡ δασεῖα κατ' ἀρχὰς τεθεῖσα ἢ μή. ἐν δὲ λόγῳ δηλονότι σύνθεσις καὶ διαίρεσις <τὸ> διττὸν ποιεῖ· δύναται δὲ κἂν τοῖς συνθέτοις τῶν ὀνομάτων αὕτη, διὰ τὸ προσεοικέναι λόγῳ, καθάπερ ἐν τῷ 'Νεάπολις' καὶ 'καλοσκἀγαθός', μεταβάλλειν τι τῶν ἁπλῶν, ἀλλ' οὐκ εἰς ἕτερον ὄνομα, τοῦτο γὰρ ἡ προσῳδία μόνη ποιεῖ,
10 ἀλλ' εἰς λόγον, ὥσπερ τὸ 'αὐλητρὶς' δηλονότι, καὶ τὸν λόγον συνθείη ποτ' ἂν εἰς ὄνομα, ὥσπερ τὸ προκείμενον. δόξει δ' οὐδὲν <ἧττον> ἄτοπον ἴσως τὸ φάσκειν διὰ τὴν προσῳδίαν τε καὶ τὴν σύνθεσιν συμβαίνειν τὰ σοφίσματα, εἴπερ ταῦτα μὲν διὰ τὸ διττόν, καθάπερ ἐλέγετο [ταῦτα] πρόσθεν, ἡ δὲ προσῳδία τε καὶ τὰ ὁμογενῆ καὶ τῶν δυνάμει διττῶν
15 ἐξαιρεῖ τὸ διττόν· ποιεῖ γὰρ ἤδη ταῦτα θάτερον σημαίνειν. καὶ λέγεται ἀληθῶς συμβαίνειν οὐδὲν ἧττον τὰ σοφίσματα διὰ ταῦτα· τῷ γὰρ τὸν λόγον ἐπιδέχεσθαι διὰ τούτων τὸ διττόν, λαβόντες θάτερον κατ' ἀρχὰς οἱ σοφισταὶ θάτερον συνάγουσι, μεταβάλλοντες μὲν διὰ τούτων τὸν

---

1 δὲ Ps.-Alex. et Anon.: τε M edd.   2 οἷον incl. Ka   δ' add. Ka   3 πρόσθεν] p. 98,7; 98,14   3 διῄρητο M   5 ὄρος ἕστηκεν MAB   6 διότι M edd.   6 συνέλθοις, καὶ αἵρεσις δὲ τὸ ποιεῖν MAB: corr. Li (*compositio et divisio duplicitatem facit*)   7 προστεθεικέναι MAB: προσεοικέναι ChK (*similia sunt* Li)   8 καλὸς κἀγαθός M edd.   μεταβάλλειν Ka: μεταβάλλοι δ' ἂν M edd.   11 ἧττον (*minus*) add. LiChK   13 ταῦτα om. ChK

14 ἡ Ka: εἰ M edd.   15 ἐξαίρει MAB   ποίει MAB   σ, M: σημαίνῃ AB: corr. Ch

not have several meanings, but signify exactly one thing. However, because it is *possible* for them to signify either of two things, they are said to be ambiguous. And this is why we say they are potential, for the potential is of this sort [namely, what is possible]. And as in our earlier division,[26] this ambiguity is either lexical or syntactic. Thus, Accent produces lexical ambiguity. For [a difference in] accent draws the word in either of two directions, as in the case of 'ορος ἕστηκεν,' [27] where [the word differs according as] the aspiration has been placed at the beginning or not.

Clearly Combination and Division produce ambiguity in the sentence, [i.e., syntactic ambiguity]. And this can occur in the case of compound words, because they resemble a sentence, for example 'Νεάπολις' ('Naples,' 'new city') and 'καλοσκἀγαθός' ('noble,' 'handsome and good'). Division is able to alter one of the simple terms, not so as to form another word, for Accent alone does this, but rather so as to form a sentence [or phrase], as is evident in 'αὐλητρίς' ('flute-girl,' 'court three times').[28] And Combination may combine the sentence into a word, as in the same example.

Now it may seem strange to claim that fallacies arise because of Accent and Combination [and Division] since these fallacies occur from ambiguity as was said earlier, whereas Accent and the like [29] serve precisely to eliminate ambiguity from what is potentially ambiguous. For Accent, and Combination and Division cause [the word or sentence] to signify just one of the two possibilities as soon [as they are applied]. And it is nevertheless true to say that the fallacies arise because of these. For [taking advantage of] the fact that the sentence admits of ambiguity by virtue of these [differences], the sophists assume at the beginning [that the premise has] one meaning, and conclude by assuming it has another, thus changing the sentence by virtue of these [namely, by virtue of Accent, Combination and Division]. For

---

[26] The division referred to is the lexical-syntactic division of actual ambiguity (into Homonymy and Amphiboly) at 98,14-16.

[27] The sentence means either 'a hill (ὅρος) stands' or 'a boundary (ὅρος) stands.'

[28] The complete example involving 'αὐλητρίς' occurs at 106,8-10.

[29] 'The like' are the other potential modes, Combination and Division. The names of the potential modes are themselves ambiguous between signifying a kind of ambiguity and signifying the disambiguating process of adding accents, and combining and dividing.

ΠΕΡΙ ΤΩΝ ΠΑΡΑ ΤΗΝ ΛΕΞΙΝ ΣΟΦΙΣΜΑΤΩΝ

λόγον, πάντως γὰρ οὐκ ἂν ἄλλως τὸ σόφισμα συμβαίη, συλλογιζόμενοι δὲ ὡς ταὐτὸ λαμβάνοντες· ὥσπερ 'ἕν τι <τὸ> λογικὸν ὄνομα, καὶ ἴδιον ἀνθρώπου· τὸ λογικὸν ἄρα ἓν ἴδιον ἀνθρώπου'· καὶ † εἰ ὅρος ἐνταῦθα στήκει ὃ τὸ χωρίον· ὅρος δ' ἐνταῦθα οὐχ ἕστηκε.' καὶ λάθοι μὲν ἂν
5 οὐδένα τὸ κίβδηλον· ἀτὰρ οὐκ ὀκνοῦσιν οἱ σοφισταὶ πανταχῇ σμικρὸν φροντίζειν τοῦ εὐλόγου· ἐπεὶ κἂν τοῖς ἐνεργείᾳ διττοῖς οὗτοί γε ταὐτὸν τοῦτο [ἕτερον] ποιοῦσι· λαβόντες γὰρ ἕτερον <ἕτερον> συλλογίζονται. ἀλλ' ἐκεῖ μὲν ἀφανέστερον, ὅτι καθ' ἑκάτερον σημαινόμενον ἂν ὁ λόγος ὁμολογηθείη, ἐνταῦθα δὲ προδήλως· διὸ καὶ <τὸ> 'τοῖς αὐτοῖς
10 ὀνόμασι καὶ λόγοις' <οὐκ ἀκριβῶς> Ἀριστοτέλης ἔφη. † οἱ μὲν γὰρ εἰσιν, οἱ τὸ εἶδος σοφισταὶ βιάζονται. ἐπεὶ δὲ ἔχομεν τὸ ἐνεργείᾳ τε καὶ δυνάμει, λείπεται <τὸ> φαντασίᾳ· τοῦτο δέ ἐστι τὸ παρὰ τὸ σχῆμα τῆς λέξεως, καθάπερ ἐλέγετο ἔμπροσθεν· φαίνοιτο γὰρ ἄν τι καὶ ὄνομα διττὸν οὐχ οὕτως ἔχον, καὶ ὁ λόγος ὁμοίως [καὶ] οὐ τοιοῦτος <ὤν. καὶ> καθ'
15 ἕκαστον τῶν προειρημένων τὰ παραδείγματα λάβοι τις ἂν ἔκ τε τῶν Εὐδήμου κἀξ ἄλλων. ἐπεὶ δ' οὖν ἔχομεν πάντας κατειλεγμένους τοὺς τρόπους, <παρ' οὓς> ἂν γένοιτό τι διττόν, ἔχομεν πάντα τὰ παρὰ τὴν λέξιν σοφίσματα· ταῦτα γὰρ οὐκ <ἂν ἄλλως συμβαίη> ἢ παρὰ τὸ διττόν· ἔχομεν δὲ καὶ τὸ [τὴν] 'τοσαυταχῶς ἂν τοῖς <αὐτοῖς>
20 ὀνόμασι καὶ λόγοις οὐ ταὐτὸν δηλώσαιμεν', ὅτι ἢ ἐνεργείᾳ ἢ

---

2 τὸ G   3 ἕν] ὂν MAB: corr. Li (*unum*)   4 λάθοι μὲν ChK (*lateret* Li): λείποιμεν ἂν MAB   5 post κίβδηλον lacuna undecim f. litter. in MA, sim. in B   7 ἕτερον om. LiChK   ἕτερον add. Ka; cf. p. 100,15 sq.   8 κατ' ἔχει σ, —ει / η M: corr. Ka; cf. Li: *quoniam quicquid significet sermo, ipsi sibi consentiat*   9 τὸ G   τοῖς αὐτοῦ MAB: αὐτοῦ τοῖς ChK   10 οὐκ ἀκριβῶς G   10-11 sensum sic restituere conatus est Ka: οἱ μὲν γὰρ εἰσιν οἱ <αὐτοὶ λόγοι. οἱ δὲ> τὸ εἶδος σοφιστικῶς βιάζονται   12 τὸ add. Ka   13 ἔμπροσθεν p. 90,2   φάναι, τί γὰρ ἄν τι καὶ ὄνομα MAB: φαίνεται γὰρ καὶ τὸ ὄνομα ChK (*ostenditur enim ipsum nomen* Li)   14 οὐ τοιοῦτος ὢν Spengel Eudemi frgm. p. 168: καὶ οὐ τοσοῦτον M edd.   καὶ add. Ka   post τοιοῦτος distinguendum esse, non post προειρημένων, ut est in M et edd., vidit Spengel ibid.   16 εὐδύμου A: εὐδήμου (non εὐδύμου) esse potest in M   κἀξ ἄλλων (ξ ἄ e corr. M¹) M. totum caput III hucusque ad Eud. libr. περὶ λέξεως refert Spengel p. 167 sq.   17 παρ' οὓς G: οἷς Prantl hist. log., p. 398 (*quibus* Li)   18 οὐκ G: οὖν MAB   ἂν ἄλλως συμβαίη G; cf. v. 1   19 ἐχόμενον M edd.   τὴν om. ChK   ἂν τοῖς] αὐτοῖς ChK αὑτοῖς G

otherwise, the fallacy would not arise at all: but the sophists draw their conclusion by supposing that the sentence is the same.

For example, in [the fallacy]: 'Rational is one word. Rational is a proprium of man. Therefore, the Rational one is a proprium of man.' And in, 'If his estate is there, then the boundary (ὄρος) stands there. A hill (ὄρος) does not stand there. Therefore, his estate is not there.'[30]

And no one would be taken in by this fraud. However, the sophists are always ready to ignore the reasonable [interpretation], for they do the very same thing even in the case of actual ambiguity: they assume [a sentence as a premise has] one meaning and conclude [supposing it has] another meaning. But in that case, [namely, in actual ambiguity] the fallacy is less obvious, because the sentence might be agreed to with either meaning, but in this case [namely, in potential ambiguity] the fraud is transparent. Hence Aristotle said, '[we mean different things] by the same words and sentences.' For some words and sentences are the same, but the sophists do violence to the form [31] [by imposing unintended meanings].

Since we have covered potential and actual ambiguity, what is left is apparent ambiguity. This is the ambiguity that arises from Form of expression, as was mentioned earlier.[32] For a word may appear to be ambiguous, when it is not, and the same may be true of a sentence. And one may take examples of each of the modes mentioned [to wit: the modes of apparent lexical and apparent syntactic ambiguity] from the works of Eudemus [33] and from other treatises.[34]

It follows that since we have enumerated all the modes from which any ambiguity arises, we have covered all the fallacies due to language. For these can only occur from ambiguity. And so we can understand [Aristotle's remark that] 'this is the number of ways in which we may fail to mean the same thing by the same words and sentences,' namely as the actual, potential, or apparent.

---

[30] The translation of this second fallacy is based on a reconstruction of Gabler's, and does not translate the text as it stands. See *infra* pp. 130-31.

[31] The translation of this sentence and the one preceding is based on an emendation of Gabler's text. See *infra* p. 131.

[32] See 90,2-7 and 98,11.

[33] On Eudemus of Rhodes, see *supra* pp. 54-55.

[34] For an example of one of these other treatises, see *supra* p. 46.

δυνάμει ἢ φαντασίᾳ· δῆλον δ' ὅτι καὶ συλλογισμοῦ τρόπον, ὁποῖόν τις ἂν προέληται, δυνατὸν ποιεῖν, ἅπαξ γε τὴν διαίρεσιν ἔχοντα, καὶ ἐξ εὐθείας καὶ εἰς τὸ ἀδύνατον ἀπάγοντα· εἰ γὰρ δυνατὸν <εἴη ὑπάρχειν ἄλλο τι διττόν>, ἀλλ' ἔσται οὔτ' ἐν ὀνόματι οὔτ' ἐν λόγῳ, οὔτ' ἐνεργείᾳ
5 οὔτε δυνάμει οὔτε φαντασίᾳ· παρὰ ταῦτα δ' οὐδὲν ὁ λόγος ἐδείκνυ. — καὶ ταῦτα μὲν ἀφωρίσθω τὸν τρόπον τοῦτον· ὅτι δ' οὐκ <ἐκ> ταὐτο<μάτου> τὴν διαίρεσιν εὑρήκαμεν, — οὐ <γὰρ> Ἀριστοτέλει χαριζόμεθα νῦν —, ἀλλὰ ταῦτα ἅπαντα κατὰ τὴν μέθοδον γέγραπται, δῆλον. τὸ μὲν γὰρ ἢ ἐν ὀνόματι δεῖν ἢ ἐν λόγῳ τὸ διττὸν εἶναι σαφῶς αὐτὸς εἴρηκεν ἐν
10 οἷς φησιν ὅτι 'τοῖς αὐτοῖς ὀνόμασι καὶ λόγοις'· τὸ <δ'> ἐνεργείᾳ ἢ δυνάμει ἢ φαντασίᾳ γνώριμον ἐκ τῆς τάξεως· γέγραπται γοῦν ἀφωρισμένα καθ' ἕκαστον εἶδος ἢ <γένος> τὰ ὁμογενῆ, καὶ πρῶτον μὲν τὰ ἐνεργείᾳ, δεύτερον δὲ τὰ δυνάμει, τρίτον δὲ τὰ φαντασίᾳ, καθάπερ δίκαιον, ἢ διὰ τί ποτ' οὐ συγκέχυται ταῦτα; ἀλλὰ γελοῖον ἴσως καὶ τὸ τῶν
15 τοιούτων ἑτέραν πίστιν πειρᾶσθαι φέρειν, μὴ τὴν ἐκ τοῦ πράγματος· εἰ γὰρ οὕτως ἔχει, καθάπερ ἡ τέχνη φησί, δηλονότι καὶ γέγονε κατ' αὐτήν, ὥσπερ ἡ ἰατρικὴ τομήν τινα οὐκ ἂν τύχῃ οὐδὲ <ἐκ> ταὐτομάτου ἐργάσαιτο. — ταῦτα μὲν οὖν ὑπὲρ τούτων ἱκανὰ πρὸς τὸ παρόν ἐστιν.

---

2 προέληται G: προσέλοιτο MAB: προέλοιτο ChK (*eligat* Li)   εἰς τὸ δυνατὸν MAB: corr. Li (*impossibile*)   3 post ἀδύνατον add. ἅπαντα τὴν διαίρεσιν ἔχοντα καὶ ἐξ εὐθείας καὶ εἰς τὸ δυνατὸν MA: dittographiam agnoverunt LiCh   ἀπάγοντες M: ἐπάγοντες AB: corr. Ch   3-4 εἴη ὑπάρχειν ἄλλο τι διττόν G: *si enim possibile est alium haberi modum* Li   4 νοήματι MAB: corr. Li (*nomine*)   5 ἐδείκνυσε (in ἐδείκνυε corr., ut vid., M¹) MAB: corr. Ch   5-6 καὶ ταῦτα G: κατ' αὐτὸ M edd.   6-7 οὐκ ἐκ ταὐτομάτου G: οὐ κατ' αὐτοὶ MAB: οὐ κατ' αὐτὸν ChK   7 γὰρ (*enim*) add. LiChK   ἄριστο M: ἀριστοτέλης AB   8 ταῦτα ἅπαντα κατὰ] κατὰ ταῦτα ἅπαντα MAB: corr. Ch   9 σαφοῦς (σαφοὺς AB) αὐτοὺς MAB: corr. Ch   10 δ' add. Ka   12 γένος om. in lac. MAB, add. ChK   πρῶτα M edd.   13 τὰ δ. edd.: τῇ δ. M   14 ἀλλ' ὡς M. edd.   15 ἑτέρα MAB: corr. Li (*aliam*)   16 ἢ φ M: φασὶ AB   17 ἐκ ταὐτομάτου G: τ'αὐτόματα MAB

And it is clear now that we can construct whichever form of syllogism one prefers [to show that there are six kinds of fallacy due to ambiguity], as long as it includes our division [i.e., the classification of the six modes], either by direct reasoning or by *reductio ad impossibile*. [The direct syllogism has been given.]³⁵ The indirect proof is equally clear.] For if it were possible for some other kind of ambiguity to exist, then it would be neither lexical nor syntactic, and not actual, potential, or apparent. But our account has shown no other ambiguity besides these.

In this way the questions which we put [namely, why there are six kinds of fallacy due to ambiguity ³⁶ and what Aristotle meant by 'some other syllogism' ³⁷] have now been determined. And it is clear that we have not found the division [of ambiguity] by chance—and we are not now doing Aristotle a favor—but it is plain that his account was methodically written. For he himself clearly said that ambiguity must lie either in the word or in the sentence when he said that it is 'by the same words and sentences [we mean different things].' And that the division is among the actual, potential, and apparent is recognizable from his ordering. For he has marked off like kinds one by one, by species or genus, and first he mentions the actual modes, second the potential, and third the apparent, as is right. Or why are these things not confounded together [in his account, if he did not have our division in mind]?

But it would perhaps be absurd even to attempt to produce some other proof of these things, other than from the subject matter itself. For if the facts [i.e., the division] stand as the art [of rational philosophy] declares, clearly they have come to be in accordance with art,³⁸ just as the art of medicine will do no cutting by chance or accidentally. This discussion of these matters is sufficient for the present.

---

[35] See *supra* p. 79.
[36] See 98,1-2.
[37] See 90,19-20. Evidently ,'the other syllogism' is the *reductio ad impossibile*.
[38] The art of Dialectic has chopped reality at the joints and laid bare the six modes of ambiguity. See *supra* p. 81.

Cap. IV. <'Επεὶ δ'> εἴρηταί τινα καὶ τοῖς Στωϊκοῖς περὶ τούτου <τοῦ> μέρους, δίκαιον ἐπελθόντα ἰδεῖν, εἴ τις ἔξω πίπτει τρόπος τῶν εἰρημένων· εἴη γὰρ <ἂν> ἐπαγωγ<ικ>ή τις αὕτη πίστις, καὶ δίκαιον ἄλλως μηδεμίαν δόξαν ἀνδρῶν εὐδοκίμων πάρεργον τίθεσθαι. τὸν μὲν
5 οὖν τῆς ἀμφιβολίας ὅρον, εἰ καὶ πρὸς πολλὰ τῶν ἡμετέρων μάχεσθαι δοκεῖ, τό γε νῦν ἐατέον, ἑτέρας γὰρ καὶ ὑπὲρ τούτων [νοσεῖν] σκοπεῖν πραγματείας· τὰς δὲ διαφορὰς τῶν λεγομένων ἀμφιβολιῶν αὐτὰς ληπτέον· εἰσί γε πρὸς τῶν χαριεστέρων λεγόμεναι τὸν ἀριθμὸν η'. μία μέν, ἣν κοινὴν ὀνομάζουσι τοῦ τε εἰρομένου καὶ τοῦ διαιρετοῦ, οἵα ἐστὶν ἡ
10 'ΑΥΛΗΤΡΙΣΠΕΣΟΥΣΑ'· κοινὴ γὰρ αὕτη τοῦ τε αὐλητρὶς ὀνόματος καὶ τοῦ <δι>ῃρημένου. δευτέρα δὲ παρὰ τὴν ἐν τοῖς ἁπλοῖς <ὁμωνυμίαν>, οἷον 'ἀνδρεῖος', ἢ γὰρ χιτὼν ἢ ἄνθρωπος· τρίτη δὲ παρὰ τὴν ἐν τοῖς συνθέτοις ὁμωνυμίαν, οἷον 'ἄνθρωπός ἐστιν'· ἀμφίβολος γὰρ ὁ λόγος, εἴτε τὴν οὐσίαν εἴτε τὴν πτῶσιν εἶναι σημαίνει. τετάρτη δέ ἐστι
15 παρὰ τὴν ἔλλειψιν, <ὡς> 'σός ἐστιν [ὡς] υἱός'· καὶ γὰρ ἐλλείπει τὸ διὰ μέσου, οἷον δεσπότου ἢ πατρός. πέμπτη δὲ παρὰ τὸν πλεονασμόν, ὥσπερ ἡ τοιαύτη 'ἀπηγόρευσεν αὐτῷ μὴ πλεῖν'· τὸ γὰρ 'μὴ' προσκείμενον ἀμφί-

---

1 Ἐπεὶ δ' add. Ka: δὲ post εἴρηται add. ChK   1-2 τούτου τοῦ G: τὸν τοῦ MAB: περὶ τούτων, <ἃ κατὰ> μέρος δίκαιον ἐπελθοῦσιν (sic ChK) ἰδεῖν ab Arnim Stoic. vet. frgm. II p. 45, 35-36   3 ἂν add. Arnim, ἐπαγωγική scrips. idem   4 μὴ δὲ μι M: μὴ δὲ μὴ AB   τίθεται MAB: corr. Li (ponere)   6 θετέον M: ἐατέον ChK: possis etiam παρετέον   νοσεῖν om. LiChK   σκοπεῖν] σκ e corr. M¹   7 πράγμα M: πράγματα AB: πραγματείας ἐστι ChK   ἀμφιβολίων MAB   8 εἰσίν MAB   λεγομένων M edd.: corr. Arnim   μίαν MAB: corr. Li (una)   9 εἰρημένου M edd.: om. AB: εἰρομένου scribend. put. Ka et Arnim l.l.   10 παῖς οὖσα MChK: om. AB, corr. Ka et Arnim   κοινὴ — αὐλητρὶς om. AB   11 εἰρημένου M edd.: διῃρημένου Ka et Arnim   δευτέρου MAB: corr. Li (altera)   ἁπλῶς M edd.: corr. Li (simplicibus)   11-12 ὁμωνυμίαν add. Arnim   12 τρίτον MAB: corr. Li (tertia)   τὴν e corr. M¹   14 τέταρτον MAB: corr. Li (quarta)   15 ὡς add. ChK (ut Li)   σός ἐστιν [ὡς] υἱός· καὶ γὰρ G: ὅ ἐστιν ὡς σοὶ καὶ ὡς MAB: ὅ ἐστί σου· καὶ γὰρ ChK   16 πέμπτον γὰρ (non δὲ) MAB: corr. Ch (quinta Li)

Chapter 4. Since the Stoics too have discussed this topic, it is right to pursue the matter and see whether any mode [of ambiguity recognized by them] falls outside those we have mentioned. This proof [that our enumeration is complete] will be inductive, and in any case it is right not to set aside any opinion of reputable men as being unimportant. Now as for their definition of amphiboly [39] which appears to conflict with many of our views, we may omit it here. For the investigation of this subject belongs to a different undertaking. But let us take up the distinctions which they make between the so-called amphibolies. The [kinds] [40] distinguished by the more subtle men of the Stoa are eight in number:

The first kind is that which they call common to what is strung along [as a continuous unit] and to what is divided; for example, 'ΑΥΛΗΤΡΙΣΠΕΣΟΥΣΑ' ('the flute-girl having fallen,' 'the court having fallen three times'). For this [kind of] ambiguity is common to 'αὐλητρίς' both as a word and as divided [into two words].

The second kind is that arising from homonymy in simple words. For example, 'manly.'[41] For either a chiton or a man is manly.

The third kind is that which arises from homonymy in compounds [of words]; for example, 'ἄνθρωπός ἐστιν' ('man is'). The sentence is ambiguous, for it signifies either that the essence or a particular [man] is.[42]

The fourth kind of ambiguity is that arising from ellipsis or omission; for example, 'the son is yours.' For the mediating term is omitted; namely, of [you as] master or [as] father.

The fifth kind is that arising from pleonasm or redundancy such as in the following: 'ἀπηγόρευσεν αὐτῷ μὴ πλεῖν' ('He forbade him to sail.' 'He forbade him not to sail'). For the 'μή' ('not') which

---

[39] The Stoics use the term 'amphiboly' as a general term for all ambiguities. Except here at 106,5 and at 106,7 it will be rendered 'ambiguity.'

[40] 'διαφοραί' is translated 'distinctions' and 'kinds.' They are the Stoic modes or types of ambiguity.

[41] 'Manly' is the translation of 'ἀνδρεῖος,' which means both 'for a man' and 'courageous.'

[42] The construction 'man is' in Greek is ambiguous in that it may mean both 'a particular man exists' and the essence (or universal) Man exists. See *supra* pp. 65-66.

ΠΕΡΙ ΤΩΝ ΠΑΡΑ ΤΗΝ ΛΕΞΙΝ ΣΟΦΙΣΜΑΤΩΝ

δοξον ποιεῖ τὸ πᾶν, εἴτε τὸ πλεῖν ἀπηγόρευσεν εἴτε τὸ μὴ πλεῖν. ἕκτην φασὶν εἶναι τὴν μὴ διασαφοῦσαν τί μετὰ τίνος ἄσημον μόριον τέτακται, ὡς ἐν τῷ 'ΚΑΙΝΥΚΕΝΗΠΑΡΕΛΑΣΣΕΝ.' τὸ γὰρ <η> στοιχεῖον <ἢ πρῶτον ἢ τελευταῖον> ἂν γένοιτο <ἢ> διαζευκτικόν. ἑβδόμη δέ
5 ἐστιν ἡ μὴ δηλοῦσα τί μετὰ τίνος τέτακται σημαντικὸν μόριον, ὡς ἐν τῷ

'Πεντήκοντ' ἀνδρῶν ἑκατὸν λίπε δῖος Ἀχιλλεύς'.

ὀγδόη <δέ ἐστιν ἡ> μὴ δηλοῦσα τί ἐπὶ τί ἀναφέρεται, ὡς ἐν τῷ 'ΔΙΩΝΘΕΩΝΕΣΤΙΝ'· ἄδηλον γάρ ἐστιν, εἴτε ἐπὶ τὴν ἀμφοτέρων ὕπαρξιν ἀναφέρεται εἴτε ἐπὶ τοιοῦτον οἷον ὁ Δίων Θέων ἐστὶν ἢ πάλιν.
10 οἱ μὲν δὴ τρόποι πρὸς τῶν χαριεστέρων οὗτοι κατηρίθμηνται. δῆλον δέ, ὅστις μὴ παρέργως τῶν ἔμπροσθεν ἤκουσεν, ὅτι πάντες πίπτουσιν εἰς τοὺς κατειλεγμένους ὑφ' ἡμῶν τρόπους, τὸ δ' ἀμέθοδόν τε καὶ ἄτεχνον πρόδηλον· οὔτε γὰρ ἐκ τῶν εἰρημένων ἀπόδειξιν <ἄν> τις λάβοι τοῦ μηδὲ καθ' ἕνα τρόπον ἕτερον ἀμφιβολόν τι δύνασθαι συστῆναι, τό τε κἂν τοῖς
15 πεπλεγμένοις ὁμωνυμίαν φάσκειν συμβαίνειν παντελῶς οὐδ' ἀκουόντων ἐστὶν ὀνομάτων. ἔτι δὲ πῶς οὐκ εὔηθες ταῖς γενικαῖς διαφοραῖς εἰδικὰς

---

1 (post πᾶν) εἴγε MABCh: corr. K   2 μὴ διασαφοῦσαν Arnim: μηδὲν σαφοῦσαν M edd.   3 καὶ νῦν καὶ μὴ παρέλασε MAB: versum restituit Arnim ex Jl. Ψ' 382   3 η G   4 ἢ πρῶτον ἢ τελευταῖον G   4 ἢ G   6 ἑκατὸν λίπε δῖος] Ἀχιλλεύς ρ̄ λείπεται MAB: rest. Ch   7 δέ ἐστιν ἡ G, pro quo spatium XIII f. litt. relictum in MAB   δηλοῦσα τί ChK: δηλονότι MAB   8 ΕΣΤΙΝ] εὕρω M: εὕρων AB: corr. Li (est)   ἄδηλος MAB: corr. Li (incertum)   9 τοιούτων MAB: corr. Ch   11 totam disputationem huius cap. huc usque ex Chrysippi περὶ ἀμφιβολιῶν libris aliquo modo pendere probabile putat ab Arnim l.l. p. 46 ann.   δέ G: γε MABCh: δέ γε K   12 ἡμῶν per comp. scriptum M: ἡμᾶς AB   13 ἄν G   13-14 μηδένα καθ' ἕνα MAB: corr. Ka   14 τι] ὄντι MAB: corr. Ch.   15 συμβαίνει MAB: corr. Li (contingere)   16 ἔστι δέ πως MAB: corr. Ka   δίκας MAB: corr. Li (speciales)

is added makes the whole ambiguous between his having forbade him to sail or not to sail.⁴³

They say that the sixth kind of ambiguity is that which fails to make clear which insignificant constituent part is construed with what. For example, 'ΚΑΙΝΥΚΕΝΗΠΑΡΕΛΑΣΣΕΝ' ('Now he [i.e., Tydeus' son] either would have passed him by [or have left the issue in doubt']).⁴⁴ For the letter η could occur as the first or as the final letter [of a word] or as a disjunctive connective.⁴⁵

The seventh kind of ambiguity is that which fails to make plain which significant constituent part is construed with what. For example, 'Πεντήκοντ' ἀνδρῶν ἑκατὸν λίπε δῖος 'Ἀχιλλεύς' ('Noble Achilles left fifty of a hundred men,' 'Noble Achilles left a hundred of fifty men').⁴⁶

The eighth kind of ambiguity is that which fails to make plain what refers to what. For example, in 'ΔΙΩΝΘΕΩΝΕΣΤΙΝ' [literally: 'Dion Theon is'], for it is unclear whether it refers to the existence of both, or to something of this sort, 'Dion is Theon' or the converse.

These are the modes which have been enumerated by the more subtle Stoics. It is obvious to anyone who has paid more than passing attention to our previous discussion that all these fall under the modes enumerated by us, and the unmethodical and unscientific character [of all this] is more than obvious. For from their account, one can find no proof that in one mode, some other [kind of] ambiguity could not be produced, and to declare that homonymy occurs even in compounds [of words] is a mark of men who have not listened to words at all.⁴⁷

Furthermore, is it not simple-minded for them to add specific

---

⁴³ After certain verbs, like 'forbid' or 'prevent,' the infinitive takes a negation (μή, not) which in Greek does not ordinarily negate the infinitive. See *supra* pp. 63-64.

⁴⁴ This verse is from *Iliad* 23. 382.

⁴⁵ It may be noted that the traditional text of Homer was written without spaces between words and it was the task of the Alexandrian scholars to establish correct word divisions. ἤ is properly read as a disjunctive connective in the sentence, but it may be taken as the first letter of a word, 'ἧπαρ' ('liver'), or the last letter of a word, 'κενή' ('void').

⁴⁶ The same example was given above at 88,18.

⁴⁷ 'ὁμωνυμία' (literally, 'sameness of name' or 'sameness of word') is derived from 'ὄνομα' ('word'). Clearly the Stoics are diverging from ordinary and Galenic usage here in taking homonymy to refer to ambiguity in a complex of words, i.e., in a sentence.

ΠΕΡΙ ΤΩΝ ΠΑΡΑ ΤΗΝ ΛΕΞΙΝ ΣΟΦΙΣΜΑΤΩΝ

<προσ>καταριθμεῖσθαι, καθάπερ ἐπὶ τῶν κατὰ τὴν διαίρεσιν ποιοῦσιν ἀσήμαντον μόριον <καὶ> σημαῖνον διαιρούμενοι· λάβοι γὰρ <ἄν τις> οὕτως γε πλείους τὰς εἰδικὰς διαφοράς· ἔτι δ' ἂν τοῦτον τὸν τρόπον τις καὶ τῆς ὁμωνυμίας ποιήσειε [δὲ] πλείους τὰς εἰδικὰς λεγομένας διαφοράς,
5 ὅτι <αἱ μὲν> αὐτῶν παρὰ τὸ ἀπὸ τύχης, αἱ δὲ παρὰ τὴν ἀναλογίαν ἢ ὁμοιότητα ἢ ἄλλον τινὰ τρόπον συνίστανται. καὶ μὲν <δὴ> καὶ τῆς ἐν λόγῳ ὁμωνυμίας ὑπ' αὐτῶν λεγομένης πλείους οἱ τρόποι, <ὧν οἱ> μὲν τῇ παραθέσει τῶν ὁμοίων πτώσεων γίγνονται, ὡς ἐν τῷ 'εἴη Μέλητον Σωκράτην νικῆσαι'· οἱ δ' ἄλλοι τρόποι <****** ἀλλὰ> ταῦτα μὲν
10 ἐλάττω, ἐκεῖνο δ' ἄξιον ἀπορίας, πῶς ποτε <παραλείπουσι τὰ> περὶ τὰς φαντασίας διττά, πολὺ δὲ μᾶλλον ἔτι, πῶς τὰ τῆς προσῳδίας· οἱ γὰρ τιθέμενοι διττοὺς [τοὺς] παρὰ τὴν <σύν>θεσιν, πῶς οὐχὶ καὶ παρὰ τὴν προσῳδίαν; ὥσπερ <γὰρ> ἐκείνη τῇ διαλήψει τοῦ ὅλου καὶ τῇ μεταξὺ σιωπῇ δύναται πρὸς τὸ διττὸν ἕλκεσθαι, οὕτω δὴ καὶ τὸ ὄνομα τῇ
15 προσῳδίᾳ· <καὶ> καθάπερ ἔξωθεν ὢν ὁ κενὸς χρόνος τοῦ λόγου καὶ οὐ μόριον αὐτοῦ διττὸν ποιεῖν αὐτὸν πέφυκεν, οὕτω δὴ καὶ ἡ προσῳδία. ἔτι δὲ καὶ οἱ σοφισταὶ καθάπερ ἐκείνῳ χρῶνται πρὸς τὰς ἔριδας, <οὕτω δὴ> καὶ ταύτῃ· καὶ μὴν αὐτὸς ἄν τις ἐφ' ἑαυτοῦ σκοπούμενος ὥσπερ ἂν παρὰ τὴν σύνθεσιν ἢ διαίρεσιν ἀμφισβητοίη, οὕτω δὴ καὶ παρὰ τὴν

---

1 προς- G   ποιουσῶν M edd.; corr. Ka   2 καὶ add. Li (et)   ἄν τις G: ἂν ChK   3 ἰδικὰς MAB: corr. Ch   τις Ka: ἧς MAB   4 ποιήσειεν MABCh   δὲ om. ABChK   πλείω τὰς αἰτίας ἀναλεγομένας MAB: πλείους εἰδικὰς λεγομένας ChK (speciales dictas plures Li)   5 αἱ μὲν add. Ka   6 συνίσταται MAB: corr. Li (constituantur)   <δὴ> G   7 ὑπ'] ἐπ' MAB: corr. Ka   ὧν οἱ add. Ka   8 Μέλητον G: μέλλει τὸν M edd.   9 σωκρα̅τ̅ M   lacunam statuit, ἀλλὰ add. Ka   10 πῶς ποτε] πώποτε MAB: πῶς ChK   παραλείπουσι add. Ka   τὰ add. ChK   11 δὴ MAB: corr. Ch   12 τοὺς eiecit Li   σύν- G   13 γὰρ (enim) add. LiChK   14 μεταξὺ Ka: μὲν M edd.   15 καὶ G   16 αὐτοῦ] ἀυ̅τ̅ M: αὐτὸν AB   δὴ] δὲ MAB: corr. Ch   17-18 οὕτω δὴ G (sic Li)   τοῦτο MAB   19 ἀμφισβητοῦσιν M edd.: corr. Ka   δὲ MAB: corr. Ch

kinds of ambiguity to the enumeration of generic kinds, as they do in their division when they divide the insignificant constituent part from the significant [i.e., in the distinction between the sixth and seventh kinds of ambiguity]. For by this procedure one can increase the number of specific kinds [further than they have]. And in this way we could also make what they call the specific kinds of homonymy greater in number, because some of them could be produced by chance, and others by analogy, or likeness or in some other manner.

And what is more, even the modes they call syntactic homonymy are several, some [examples] of which arise by juxtaposition of similar cases [of the noun], as in 'εἴη Μέλητον Σωκράτην νικῆσαι' ('May Socrates prevail over Meletus.' 'May Meletus prevail over Socrates').[48] And the other modes * * * but these are fewer.[49] And this is worth puzzling over, how in the world they omit the [kinds of] ambiguity due to appearance,[50] and even more so, how they omit the ambiguity due to Accent. For how can those who recognize ambiguity due to Combination fail to recognize ambiguity due to Accent? For just as the former case [catalogued as Combination] can be drawn toward ambiguity by separation of the whole, namely by silence [i.e., pause or break] in between [the words], so the word is drawn toward ambiguity by accentuation.[51] And just as the empty time [i.e., the pause] which is outside the sentence and not a constituent part is of such a nature as to make it ambiguous, so also in the case of accentuation.

[There is a further support for this parallel.] Just as the sophists use the word break [or pause] in disputation to produce ambiguity, so too do they use accentuation. Even a man considering a matter by himself [52] might hesitate in regard to Combination or Division, and similarly he might hesitate in regard to Accent. This is clear

---

[48] In Greek, both 'Socrates' and 'Meletus' are in the accusative case, and each can be taken as either subject or object of the infinitive 'to prevail over.'

[49] The translation is admittedly incoherent and reflects a lacuna in Galen's text.

[50] The kinds due to appearance are the apparent modes of ambiguity, Form of expression (L) and Form of expression (S).

[51] 'Accentuation' here is the rendering of 'προσῳδία,' which is usually translated 'Accent.' This rendering reflects the ambiguity of the Greek. See *supra* p. 100*, n. 29.

[52] A man who considers a matter by himself here is one who is reading an unaccented or undivided text.

προσῳδίαν· δῆλον δὲ ἐπὶ τῶν γεγραμμένων λόγων, οἷς μὴ πρόσκειται διακρίνοντα σημεῖα· δεῖται γὰρ ὥσπερ ἐκείνων εἰς τὴν διάκρισιν, οὕτω δὴ καὶ τῆς προσῳδίας, οὐκ ἀεί γε μήν· καὶ δι' αὐτὴν <ἄρ'> ἐγίγνετο διττὸς ὁ λόγος.

1 οἷς ChK: θεὶς MAB   2 διακρίνειν τὰ MAB: corr. Li (*dividentia*)   3 δή] δὲ MAB   μήν ChK: μὴ MAB   fort. διὰ ταύτην   ἄρ' G   γένοιτο ChK

in the case of written sentences in which word division signs and accentual marks have not been added. For just as the written sentence requires these signs [or spaces] for dividing the words, so it needs the accentual marks, though not in every case. Therefore, by virtue of Accent too, as we have seen, the sentence becomes ambiguous.

PART THREE
TEXTUAL COMMENTARY

CHAPTER TEN

HISTORICAL AND TEXTUAL COMMENTARY

88,2-6. As it occurs both in the title and in the first sentence, 'παρά' with the accusative seems to be interchangeable with 'διά' in the same construction, meaning 'due to,' 'on account of,' or 'by.' On the 'causal παρά' see Smyth (*Greek Grammar*, p. 382, sec. 1692, 3c).

88,5. The term 'τρόπος' ('mode') seems to be ambiguous here between signifying a type of fallacy (i.e., a species of apparent argument due to language) and a mode of ambiguity (i.e., a species of linguistic ambiguity which causes and denominates its corresponding fallacy). A mode of ambiguity is logically prior to (that is, may occur independently of) any fallacy. A fallacy is an argument consisting of one or more premises (sentences) that appear to entail another sentence (the conclusion), but actually do not. Since Galen gives as examples of the various modes only cases of ambiguous sentences, presumably a mode here is just the linguistic phenomenon of sentential ambiguity that causes the fallacies *in dictione*.

88,7. 'σχῆμα (τῆς) λέξεως,' which I render 'Form of expression,' is sometimes rendered as 'Figure of Speech.' For example, see Joseph (*Introduction to Logic*, p. 543).

88,10. As it occurs here, 'ἀμφιβολία' is used in its technical sense to denote grammatical ambiguity. But 'ἀμφιβολία' is also a general term for ambiguity: See Aristotle *Poetica* 25. 1461^{a}25-26, and the Stoic usage at Diog. Laert. 7. 62. In Chapter 4 of *De Captionibus* Galen uses the term 'ἀμφιβολία' to specify the general notion of ambiguity in describing the Stoic teaching.

88,11. Gabler's text for the example of Amphiboly, following the Ambrosian MS., 'γένοιτο καταλαβεῖν τὸν ὗν ἐμέ,' seems to be right. This sentence is similar in its structural ambiguity to Aristotle's example (*Soph. El.* 4. 166^{a}6-7), and is identical with the illustration of Amphiboly that occurs in Ps.-Alexander's *Commentarius* (p. 138, l. 12). The ambiguity arises in the example because each of the two accusatives may be construed either as the subject or as the object of the infinitive 'καταλαβεῖν.' Little is known about Ps.-Alexander except that he is an Aristotelian commentator who knew Galen's work *De Captionibus*. Indeed, Galen's name occurs twice in his commentary (p. 22, l. 7, and p. 142, l. 29). F. Edward Cranz, in his article 'Alexander Aphrodisiensis,' (in *Catalogus Translationum et Commentariorum: Mediaeval and Renaissance Latin Translations and Commentaries*, ed. by Paul Oskar Kristeller, Vol. I (Washington, D.C.: Catholic University of America Press, 1960), p. 79), informs us that Alexander's commentary on Aristotle's *Sophistici Elenchi* is lost, but that the extant commentary of Ps.-Alexander has been preserved with the genuine commentaries of Alexander. Cranz disagrees with Wallies (the editor of the critical edition of 1898) who claims that the Ps.-Alexander is Michael of Ephesus. On this dispute, see Cranz, pp. 124-25.

88,13. Presumably Galen includes as accentuation (the process of placing some accent mark or other, or the mark itself) breathings (rough and smooth) in addition to accents themselves (acute, grave, and circumflex). If he did not, then 'ορος' would be ambiguous between 'ὄρος' and 'ὀρός' (between 'hill' and 'whey')—and this would render unintelligible Galen's example of the fallacy Accent at *102,3-4*. For in that case Galen would be construing 'ὀρός' ('whey') with 'ἵστημι' ('stands'). At *102,3-4* it seems clear that we are warranted in taking Galen to be referring to the ambiguity between 'ὄρος' and 'ὅρος,' and to recognize breathings as a form of accentuation for him. Hence for Galen προσῳδία as pitch accent accompanying the word to which it is attached, is extended to include the rough and smooth breathing, the former being pronounced as *H* before certain initial vowels, diphthongs, and the initial rho. Kalbfleisch's suggestion, accepted by Gabler, of substituting 'δασεῖαν' for 'διττήν' at *88,15* seems warranted then.

For Aristotle the case seems just as obvious. However, A. N. Jannaris (in 'Plato's Testimony to Quantity and Accent,' *American Journal of Philology* XXIII (1902), 76-77), argues that προσῳδία for Aristotle refers strictly to tone (pitch) and not breathing. And hence Jannaris claims that the ambiguity of 'ορος' (at *Soph. El.* 20. 177ᵇ3-4) is between 'ὄρος' and 'ὀρός.' On this see *supra* p. 28, n. 60. Jannaris' reading of *De Captionibus* and his ascription of the same position to Galen, however, is unconvincing, in view of the considerations advanced above.

88,14. 'διπλοῦν' appears to be a mere stylistic variant of 'διττόν,' and hence, means 'ambiguity.' Galen seems to be concerned with his own style here; specifically, he wants to avoid reiteration of the same word 'διττόν.' It may be noted that in general, Galen's Attic prose is marred by redundancy and digression, and Galen is known for his tendency toward longwindedness, even in antiquity. For example, Simplicius refers to our philosopher as 'ὁ φιλολογώτατος Γαληνός' ('the most talkative Galen' or 'the most discourse-loving Galen') with a pun on 'φιλόλογος' meaning 'student of literature,' and hence, 'philogist,' (in *In Aristotelis Physicorum Libros Quattuor Posteriores Commentaria*, ed. by H. Diels, (Berlin: *C.I.A.G.*, 1895), Vol. X, Pts. 5-8, p. 1039, l. 13).

88,15-16. Here Galen treats the two distinct Aristotelian modes, Combination and Division, as a unity. Ps.-Alexander observes that Galen combines these two modes and justifies his observation by quoting these lines of *De Captionibus* verbatim (*Commentarius*, p. 142, ll. 29-31). For here Galen refers to Combination and Division by a singular term 'αὕτη.' This grammatical evidence is supported by philosophical evidence provided in Chapter 3. There Galen defines Combination and Division by the same genus and differentia.

88,16-17. 'ἡ τοῦ σημαινομένου διαφορά' ('the difference in what is meant') seems to be yet another expression synonymous with 'διττόν.' This variant suggests Stoic terminology that Galen has inherited. One Stoic term for 'meaning' is 'σημαινόμενον' (see Diog. Laert. 7. 62).

88,18. Galen's example of Combination and Division is identical with one that falls under Aristotle's heading Division (*Soph. El.* 4. 166^{a}37-38): 'Πεντήκοντ᾽ ἀνδρῶν ἑκατὸν λίπε δῖος Ἀχιλλεύς.' What its two senses are precisely is not immediately clear. The Oxford translation renders it 'God-like Achilles left fifty a hundred men.' The Loeb translation reads 'goodly Achilles left a hundred (and) fifty men.' Neither of these renderings of the sentence comes to grips with the occurrence of 'ἄνδρες' in the genitive case. Following Ps.-Alexander, (*Commentarius*, p. 32, ll. 12-16) we may say that the ambiguity depends on where we put a comma (ὑποστίζω) in the example. If we place it after the first word, 'πεντήκοντα,' the sentence may be rendered 'Noble Achilles left behind fifty of one hundred men.' The placement of the comma in this way (or of pause if the sentence is uttered) clearly indicates that 'πεντήκοντα' ('fifty') is to be construed as object of the verb 'λείπω,' and 'ἑκατόν' ('one hundred') is to be taken as partitive genitive with 'ἄνδρες' ('men'). If the comma (or pause) is placed after 'ἀνδρῶν,' however, then the sentence may be rendered 'Noble Achilles left behind one hundred of fifty men.' In this case, 'πεντήκοντα' as partitive genitive is construed with 'ἄνδρες,' and 'ἑκατόν' is taken as object of the verb. Admittedly the second sense of the example is arithmetically impossible, but Aristotle tolerates cases of ambiguity in which one of the senses is absurd; e.g., 'ἐπίσταται γράμματα' ('he has knowledge of letters.' 'letters have knowledge,' at *Soph. El.* 4. 166ᵃ18-21).

90,1. Gabler's text, which includes the Charterian addition of 'συντιθεμένου ἤ' seems to capture Galen's meaning. This reading is corroborated by Ps.-Alexander (*Commentarius* p. 32, ll. 10-12). Gabler also follows the Charterian reading of 'τοῦ' for 'τῶν' before 'ἀνδρῶν' by which we take Galen to be speaking in the formal rather than in the material mode—that is, to be speaking of the word 'ἄνδρες,' rather than of ἄνδρες. For the sake of consistency I emend the text at 90,1, substituting 'τοῦ' for 'τῶν,' and hence keep Galen in the formal mode. It is the word '50,' not 50, that is being construed together with or separately from the word 'ἄνδρες.'

90,4-5. Gabler has daggered the text after 'σχῆμα,' and I emend 90,5 in conformity with a suggestion he includes in the apparatus criticus:

σχῆμα· παραπλησία γάρ ἐστι τοῖς τοῦ ποιεῖν, τῷ τρέχω καὶ νοῶ·

Taken in this way, 'ὅπερ ἐστὶ τὸ σχῆμα' becomes a clause whose function is to clarify the sense of 'προφορά,' a technical term which seems to be a staple in the Stoic theory of language. The term does not occur in Aristotle anywhere according to the *Index Aristotelicus* (ed. by H. Bonitz, in *Aristotelis Opera*, Vol. V. (Berlin: Academica Regia Borussica, 1870), but the Stoics specify by 'προφορά' articulate utterance; that is, the outward expression of language, which does not necessarily mean anything. Even parrots are said to be capable of προφορικὸς λόγος (Sext. Emp. *Adv. Math.* 8. 275). On the difference between λέγειν and προφέρεσθαι see Diog. Laert. 7. 57, and on the use of the term 'προφορά' see Sext. Emp. *Pyrrhoneiae Hypotyposes* 1. 15. 203. For Galen, προφορά is the formal vehicle by which the meaning of a word can be expressed and conveyed, and hence, the exegetical nature of the remark in this passage, to the effect that προφορά is the *form* of the word.

A further virtue of this emendation of 90,5 is that it eliminates the problematic occurrence of 'κρατεῖσθαι' ('to be governed'), whose sense does not fit the context. Galen's point seems clear—that a verb like 'ἀκούω' is similar in form to verbs specifying activity (i.e., its form is that of an active verb).

90,10-13. Here Galen quotes what he takes to be a λόγος (argument) in the *Soph. El.* (4. 165ᵇ27-30), by which Aristotle proves that his list of fallacies *in dictione* is exhaustive:

> To show this, there is a proof by induction and a syllogism, (and perhaps there is some other syllogism that may be taken), that this is the number of ways in which we may fail to mean the same thing by the same words and sentences.

This passage is ambiguous in that the final clause may be construed either in apposition with the initial 'this' in the sentence ('τούτου' in Greek) or with the first occurrence of 'syllogism' ('συλλογισμός'). Construed in the first way, the final clause may be understood as the conclusion which the inductive and deductive proofs will draw. But construed in the second way, the final clause is taken as specifying the deductive proof, that is, the entire syllogism. And Galen's remarks at 90,19-92,1 indicate that he interprets Aristotle as saying that the final clause represents a complete syllogism, whereas as Galen points out, in fact it is nothing but a syllogistic conclusion. Although Galen's reading of this passage is uncharitable and even perverse, he at once absolves Aristotle for this imprecision on the grounds that brevity is a common feature of Aristotle's writing, especially when he is writing for those who have already heard his doctrines expounded.

It may be noted that the last clause of the passage in question seems to provide the basis for Galen's implicit intuitive definition of ambiguity in this treatise—διττόν is the failure of the same word or sentence to mean the same thing.

90,23. As early as Galen, Aristotle seems to be referred to by the honorific title, ὁ φιλόσοφος.

92,11. It may be noted that Ps.-Alexander reconstructs Galen's line of reasoning in the following way (*Commentarius* p. 22, ll. 8-22):

> (1) The fallacies due to language occur from the failure by the same words and sentences to signify the same things.
> (2) All the fallacies occurring from the failure by the same

words and sentences to signify the same things happen to be six.

∴ (3) All the fallacies due to language happen to be six.

Ps.-Alexander offers the following 'prosyllogism' to prove premise (1) above:

(4) Fallacies due to language arise from vice in language.
(5) All fallacies arising from vice in language occur from the failure by the same words and sentences to signify the same things.

∴ (1) The fallacies due to language occur from the failure by the same words and sentences to signify the same things.

Clearly the above argument for (1) is a simplified version of the Galenic argument in Chapter 2 of *De Captionibus*. (The complete structure and content of Galen's line of reasoning there is described in the analysis given *supra* pp. 72-74.)

92,14. Here for the first time Galen refers directly to the 'sophists' (rather than to 'sophistical arguments' as at *90,6*). It seems clear that Galen is not specifying any contemporaries of his, the members of the so-called Second Sophistic, one of whom was Aristides Aelius, whom Galen once met. Such sophists of the second century A.D. were primarily rhetoricians. On this subject, see G. W. Bowersock, *Greek Sophists in the Roman Empire* (Oxford: Clarendon Press, 1969), pp. 8, 62.

The sophists Galen is referring to at *92,14*, on the other hand, are men who argue unscrupulously for any conclusion, like Dionysodorus and Euthydemus in Plato's *Euthydemus*. For Galen, a sophist is a man who depends on sophistical premises to draw his conclusion, and a typical sort of sophistical premise is one that consists of an ambiguous sentence. For example, in *De Placitis 2* (Müller ed.) Vol. I, p. 212, ll. 2-5, Galen refers to an ambiguous premise used by Zeno (the founder of Stoicism), to show that the mind is not in the brain. Galen writes, 'Now if Zeno was aware of this fraud and made use of it intentionally, he would be a sophist, not a philosopher; if he used it in ignorance and unintentionally, his training in logic was deficient,' (DeLacy translation). This passage in *De Placitis* clearly supports the claim that for Galen, the sophists are men who intentionally use spurious arguments. This is also Aristotle's view. See *Rhet.* I. I. 1355^{b}17-18, 'What makes a man a 'sophist' is not his faculty, but his moral purpose' (Oxford translation).

92,18. Kalbfleisch's addition of 'κακία' here is surely warranted by the sense—*Vice* is the failure of the corresponding virtue. Though not an exact quotation from any of the dialogues, this principle is of course Platonic. For example, at *Resp*. 1. 353b1-353c4, the eyes' proper virtue is said to be sight and their proper vice blindness; clearly the latter would be the 'failure' of the former. 'Failure' here means 'negation' or 'privation.'

92,19-20. Galen states that the principle, 'The excellence and the virtue of anything are in its function,' has been proved (ἀποδείκνυμι) in other discussions, but it is unclear what these are. Gabler does not justify his ascription of these discussions to Galen (in 'Index Nominum,' p. 36 of the Gabler edition, where 'ἐν ἑτέροις λόγοις' is listed under the entry *Galenus*).

92,20. 'πρὸς ὃ πέφυκεν ἢ γέγονεν' is literally 'that for which a thing is suited by nature or that for which a thing has come into being,' and it is rendered 'function' in the translation beginning at *92,21-22*. Galen's language here resembles Plato's, especially at *Resp*. 10. 601d5-6, where Plato writes:

> And . . . the excellence or beauty or rightness of any implement or living creature or action has reference to the use for which it is made or designed by nature (πεποιημένος ἢ πεφυκός), (Cornford translation).

The pairs of verbs ποιοῦμαι—φύω, γίγνομαι—φύω, seem to point to the observance of the same distinction between the object in question being natural (a man at *92,20*, an eye at *94,5*), or not (a blade at *92,21*, a pipe for Plato at *Resp*. 10. 601e1). In this way, πρὸς ὃ πέφυκεν specifies the function of natural objects, whereas πρὸς ὃ γέγονεν refers to the function of artifacts.

That Galen preserves this awkward locution (*91,21-22*; *94,7*) even in regard to language is a sign that he does not wish to run afoul of the νόμος-φύσις controversy, insofar as it bears on the nature of language in this introductory treatise on ambiguity and fallacy due to language. Taking either side on the question of the origin of language, would obscure more than it would illuminate these topics. External evidence suggests, however, that Galen adheres to the position that language is an artifact, or exists by convention in the sense that there is no natural connection between names and what they signify. For example, in *De Methodo Medendi* 1 (Kühn ed.) Vol. X, p. 45, Galen recommends that a speaker *fix* the meanings of his terms at the beginning of a discourse as a requirement of its being methodical.

It may be mentioned that Galen's catalogue of his works (*De Libris Propriis* (Kühn ed.) Vol. XIX, pp. 43-48), fails to include any title for a work devoted to the topic of nature-convention in regard to language. Perhaps the controversy seemed to Galen to be a red herring, or to be resolved by Aristotle (*De Int.* 2. 16ª19), and reopened wrongly in favor of 'nature' by the Stoics. (The Stoic writings contain etymological entries with some frequency. Appeals to the genesis of a word often support philosophical theses for them (see Diog. Laert. 7. 108; 114; 147). Galen's custom is to inquire into the usage of a term, not into its linguistic history. For an example, see Galen's *De Animi Peccatis Dignoscendis* 2 (*Scripta Minora*) Vol. II, p. 45, ll. 4-9.

92,22. The force of the 'φαίνομαι' here is not to indicate hesitation or doubt that the function of language is to signify, but rather to suggest the following: that when you think about it, sure enough, signifying is the one function of language.

94,1. Here Galen asserts that the excellence and poor quality of a thing are in its function. Galen's language (and corresponding conceptual apparatus) parallels both Plato's at *Resp.* 1 and Aristotle's at *E.N.* 1. 7. 1097ᵇ24-1098ª20. At *Resp.* 1. 353b2-3, in an exchange between Socrates and Thrasymachus, it is agreed that each thing that has a function (ἔργον) has a virtue, and Socrates induces Thrasymachus to assent to the following: '... that there is always some specific virtue which enables them [sc. things with a function] to work well (εὖ); and if they are deprived of that virtue, they work badly (κακῶς),' (*Resp.* 1. 353c6-7, Cornford translation).

94,3. I have rendered 'εὐαρμοστία' as 'sonority' in the translation. It occurs at *Resp.* 3. 400d11-400e1, where Socrates states that 'excellence of form and content in discourse and of musical expression (εὐαρμοστία) and rhythm, and grace of form and movement, all depend on goodness of nature....' (Cornford translation). 'εὐαρμοστία' would appear to be the good musical quality that is present in language especially suited to being sung; indubitably among modern languages Italian would qualify as being such. Sonority is a virtue of language *qua* sound, not *qua* signifier. The other accidental virtue of language, calligraphy, consists of its being written in an attractive manner, and is the virtue of language *qua* system of inscriptions.

94,7. The translation is based on an addition of 'τοῦτο' before 'πρός' at *94,7*. By breviloquy Galen here identifies the virtue of a thing and that thing's function, 'τοῦτο πρὸς ὃ πέφυκεν ἢ γέγονεν.' The ellipse is acceptable given the formula Galen states at *92,20*. Of course, what Galen means is that the virtue of a thing resides in its proper function.

94,8. Gabler's conjecture 'λάβοι' at *94,8* is as dubious as the Charterian and Kühn addition of 'γνοίη,' since the hiatus resulting from *both* emendations is of a type not countenanced by Galen, (see Gabler, pp. xiii-xiv, and Galen, *Institutio Logica* (Kalbfleisch ed.), p. viii). Because the sense of the passage warrants 'λάβοι,' I accept Prof. DeLacy's suggestion to insert 'λάβοι' after 'ἄν' and before 'τις,' (i.e., as 'ἄν λάβοι τις,'), thus preventing the hiatus. There is a parallel to this in *De Placitis* 3 (Müller ed.) Vol. I, p. 271, namely 'ἄν ἔχοι τις.'

94,11. Gabler's addition at *94,11*, 'ἀνήκει, κακία τῆς λέξεως ἔσται τὸ' makes sense of the text and of Galen's overall line of argument in Chapter 2. The hiatus produced is of a sort allowed by Galen (namely, after vowels that admit elision). On this see, Gabler, pp. xiii-xiv, and Galen, *Institutio Logica* (Kalbfleisch ed.), p. viii.

96,1. 'διάλεκτος' here refers to a foreign language; i.e., any language that conveys meaning for members of one linguistic community but not for members of another. Persian and Ethiopian, though bona fide languages, do not signify 'for us' Galen explains, and are hence foreign languages. The notion of a word being foreign 'for us' is present in Aristotle (*Poet.* 21. 1457^{b}1-6), who claims that the word 'σίγυνον' is an ordinary word in Cyprus, but is foreign (γλῶττα), (and presumably insignificant) for us.

96,3. If we accept Gabler's emendation 'ποιοῦμεν κρίσιν,' then Galen is saying that the reason why we can declare one insignificant language (for us) superior to another is that we are making a judgment of φωνή (sound) rather than of λέξις (language). Here we find that Galen's distinction between sound and language *qua* signifier coincides with the Stoic distinction between sound (φωνή) or articulate sound (λέξις), and language which signifies (λόγος). See Diocles of Magnesia in Diog. Laert. 7. 57, (also, SVF III, p. 213, #20).

96,4-5. The Kalbfleisch additions of 'τῷ,' 'κακίαν,' and '-το' make sense of this passage. Here Galen is grinding one of his favorite axes, claiming that this error (of mistaking 'not signifying' for 'not signifying well' as the vice of language) results from a failure to distinguish unlike things which happen to resemble each other in certain respects. This error is pointed out by Plato (*Phaedrus* 262b2-3), and Galen cites it, for example, in his *De Animi Peccatis Dignoscendis* 2 (*Scripta Minora*) Vol. I, p. 48):

> The large number of [philosophical] sects makes it clear that some charlatans are winning disciples; it is also clear that these charlatans would not have convinced anybody to accept their teachings as true unless they bore a certain similarity to the truth. Nor should we think that this similarity is a slight one.

(The translation of this passage is by Paul Harkins, in *Galen On the Passions and Errors of the Soul* (Columbus: Ohio State University Press, 1963), p. 76.)

96,7-8. The Limanus, Charterian, Kühn, and Gabler addition of 'μή' at *96,7* is needed to make the passage and the argument in it intelligible. By 'ὅτι' in *96,8* Galen seems to recognize ambiguity as the formal cause of signifying well. The force of *96,7-8* is to indicate that signifying ambiguously is what we mean by signifying poorly.

96,10-14. As Gabler notes in his apparatus, the principle at *96,11-12*, 'Every corruptible thing is corrupted by its own vice,' is based on *Resp.* 10. 609A-C, where Plato tries to prove that the soul is immortal by showing that if injustice, the proper vice of the soul, cannot *destroy* it, no other vice can. (I render 'φθείρω' by 'to corrupt,' and 'διαφθείρω' by 'to destroy.') Plato's point is that the soul is corrupted by injustice, but not destroyed by it. Clearly then Galen is diverging from the Platonic premise. If he were faithful to it, then 'not signifying' would be the vice of language, for it destroys language on Galen's theory. Hence, though he appeals to Platonic authority in proposing an independent argument to show that ambiguity is the vice of language, Galen alters the Platonic principle he is invoking.

96,16. 'ἔνδεια' ('elliptical utterance') is the opposite of redundance. On this, see Apollonius Dyscolus *Syntax* 133. 15. 'μακρολογία' ('prolixity') occurs in Plato (*Gorgias* 449c5) and in Aristotle (*Rhet.* 3. 17. 1418^{b}24).

98,3-4. After the dagger, rather than 'ἐκ λόγων' I read Gabler's suggestion of 'ἐκ τίνων,' and the translation is based on this emendation. The sense is natural, for Galen is asking of what a sentence consists, a question which is answered at *98,5-6*.

98,4. 'πρότασις' is, of course, the Aristotelian term for premise. See *An. Pr.* I. 1. 24^{a}16 and I. 25. 42^{a}32-33. But in other places, notably his *Institutio Logica* 4. 8, and 20. 5, Galen prefers the Stoic term for premise, 'λῆμμα.' See Diog. Laert. 7. 45, 77.

98,5-6. Clearly Galen's syntactic analysis of a sentence is oversimplified for the purpose at hand. In the *Institutio Logica* 2. 2-3, Galen gives a more thorough description of a premise in terms of subject, predicate, and auxiliary (ἐπίρρημα), which is the copula in that context. We recall previous definitions of the sentence in Greek philosophy: At *Sophist* 262c9-262d4 the Stranger induces Theaetetus to agree that 'A man understands' is a λόγος of the first (simplest) and shortest kind, because 'now it gives information about facts or events in the present or past or future: it does not merely name something but gets you somewhere by weaving together (συμπλέκω) verbs with names' (Cornford translation). In the *Cratylus* Plato describes a sentence as a composite of names (ὀνόματα) and verbs (ῥήματα), (425A). For other Platonic remarks on the sentence, see *supra* p. 37, n. 21.

At *De Int.* 4. 16^{b}26, Aristotle defines a λόγος (meaning 'phrase') as 'significant sound, of which some part is significant in separation,' and at *Poet.* 20. 1457^{a}23, as 'composite significant sound, of which some parts signify something by themselves.' He defines a *declarative* sentence (ἀποφαντικὸς λόγος) as one which may be true or false (*De Int.* 4. 17^{a}2-3), which must include a verb (*De Int.* 5. 17^{a}10), and which signifies concerning some subject whether some attribute belongs to it or not (*De Int.* 5. 17^{a}23-24).

Dionysius Thrax states that a λόγος is a combination of words that makes plain a complete thought, (if we read 'λέξεων' for 'λέξεως'), in *Ars Grammatica*, ed. G. Uhlig, p. 22, l. 5.

And Ps.-Alexander (*Commentarius*, p. 28, l. 8) seems to lift his definition of a sentence straight from *De Captionibus*, saying that a sentence is a combination of ὀνόματα. Plainly Galen's definition is most akin to those of Plato (as a composite of nouns and verbs), and less so to those of Aristotle and the grammarian Dionysius Thrax.

The problem in rendering some of the grammatical terms that

occur at 98,5-6 has been pointed out by P. B. R. Forbes, in 'Greek Pioneers in Philology and Grammar,' *Classical Review* XLVII (July, 1933), 109: 'In all such discussions by the pioneers in grammar a just translation is difficult since the terms in the Greek (like ὄνομα) are everyday words, whereas in English 'noun' means nothing outside the grammar-school.'

98,7. 'διὰ τὸ γνωριμώτερον' may also be rendered 'because names (i.e., nouns and adjectives) are the more familiar form of words,' but this does not seem right, for verbs are just as 'familiar' in language as nouns and adjectives. In any case, Galen is bowing to 'ordinary' Greek parlance by using 'ὀνόματα' to cover all words. Prof. DeLacy has pointed out to me that when there is a conflict between popular usage and medically justified usage, Galen often accepts the former. For example, the carotid arteries (καρωτίδες) have nothing to do with κάρος (stupefaction), but Galen uses the term 'καρωτίδες' anyway. See *De Placitis* 1 (Müller ed.) Vol. I, p. 151 and *De Placitis* 2 (Müller ed.) Vol. I, pp. 228-29. In this passage in *De Captionibus* Galen seems to be accepting ordinary usage in spite of the fact that it means that a verb is called an ὄνομα.

98,9-10. Although the text here is corrupt, the occurrence of the terms 'λίθος' and 'συγκείμενον' ('stone' and 'composite') warrants the claim that Galen is appealing to an architectural analogy. Analogies with houses or house building, perhaps reflecting the fact that his father was an architect, are not uncommon in Galen. See his *De Constitutione Artis Medicae ad Patrophilum* (Kühn ed.) Vol. I, p. 227 (cited by Gilbert, p. 17). The occurrence of these two terms is consistent with Kalbfleisch's proposed addition, which is included in the Gabler apparatus. Hence *98,9-10* would read as follows: 'ἔχοι κατ' οἰκίαν κακὸν οὐδὲν ἐνδείκνυσθαι παρ' ἕκαστα τῶν λίθων ἢ τὸ συγκείμενον.' The lexical-syntactic distinction in a sentence is similar to the case of a house where there is nothing one can find fault with besides the stones taken severally, or the composite, the structure of the house as a whole.

It is clear that a sentence that is ambiguous in only one way cannot be both lexically and syntactically ambiguous. Borderline cases do crop up, however, that Galen does not adjudicate in this respect. For example, the sentence, 'The violinist was poor,' (Quine, *Word and Object*, p. 134). One might claim that it is simply a case of lexical ambiguity, 'poor' meaning 'impoverished' and 'of inferior quality.' However, Quine holds that such ambiguity is syntactic. What is ambiguous in that case is the predicative position as between being truly predicative and syncategorematic (Quine, p. 134).

98,12. For the identity of these other discussions, see *supra* pp. 54-55.

98,13-16. As Gabler point out in his apparatus, Ps.-Alexander (*Commentarius*, p. 22, l. 3 to p. 23, l. 2) quotes Galen's *98,13-16* nearly verbatim. The major difference is that 'ὁ' at *98,14* anaphorically refers to one of οἱ εἰρημένοι τρόποι (*98,13* 'the modes of ambiguity'), whereas Ps.-Alexander speaks of οἱ σοφισμοί as being actually ambiguous.

100,4-6. According to the Ambrosian MS. and the Aldine and Basel editions, Galen's example of the mode Accent is ὄρος ἔστηκεν, with smooth breathings and acute accents over the first letter of each word (*100,5*). That these texts are at least partially corrupt is immediately suggested from the fact that there is no such word as 'ἔστηκεν' in Greek. The word intended is clearly 'ἕστηκεν.' The problem with the example is that it is singularly unambiguous as stated in these editions; it means precisely one thing, 'a hill stands' whether it is written or spoken. But in this passage, Galen is saying that a difference in accentuation (which includes breathings) 'draws the word in either of two directions' (as in the case of 'ορος ἕστηκεν'). And it seems that what this difference in accentuation operates on is the unaccented unit 'ορος'—hence, I accept the Kühn, Gabler formulation of Galen's example of Accent, 'ορος ἕστηκεν.'

100,6-11. When the ambiguity of a sentence is due to the occurrence of 'Νεάπολις' ('Naples'), 'καλοσκἀγαθός' ('noble'), and 'αὐλητρίς' ('flute-girl', an example of Stoic origin, see Diog. Laert. 7. 62, and *106,10*), these sentences are syntactically ambiguous. Written in *scriptura continua* or pronounced indistinctly without pause these units resemble the phrases 'Νέα πόλις' ('new city'), 'καλὸς κἀγαθός' ('handsome and good'), and 'αὐλὴ τρίς' ('a court three times'). Admittedly such cases of Combination and Division, (when spoken without pause and clearly enunciated as such) may be taken as combined rather than divided, and hence as unambiguous. But this only suggests that these are bad examples of Combination and Division. The paradigmatic case of this mode is the sentence which when distinctly articulated without pause remains ambiguous, like, 'Πεντήκοντ' ἀνδρῶν ἑκατὸν λίπε δῖος Ἀχιλλεύς' (*88,18*).

100,18. 'θάτερον' may be rendered 'another meaning.' Cf. *100,15* and *102,8*.

102,2-3. The text for the example of Combination and Division is corrupt in the tradition, and the Limanus correction of 'ἕν' for 'ὄν' at *102,3*, and the Gabler insertion of 'τό' at *102,2* seem acceptable. However, Gabler's reconstruction of the fallacy, 'verbum τὸ λογικὸν est unum; τὸ λογικὸν proprium est hominis: componit sophista concludens τὸ λογικὸν esse unum proprium hominis neques aliis rebus eum a ceteris distingui,' is not persuasive in that it depends on an artifice in the reading of the conclusion. See Gabler, 'Observationes,' pp. 23-24. That is, Gabler's reconstruction of Galen's example would read as follows in English:

(1) The word 'Rational' is one (thing).
(2) The Rational is a proprium of man.
∴ (3) The Rational is (the) one proprium of man (*102,2-3*

The artifice is the inclusion of the (equivalent of the) definite article, that is, concluding that Rational is the one and only proprium of man. The rendering included in the translation (*supra* p. 102*) is a better reading of the Greek, and the conclusion it draws is completely unreasonable, a characteristic feature of sophistic argumentation.

In Greek, the conclusion is 'τὸ λογικὸν ἄρα ἓν ἴδιον ἀνθρώπου.' If it is divided after 'λογικόν,' then 'ἕν' is combined with 'ἴδιον ἀνθρώπου,' and as such may be rendered 'The Rational is one proprium of man.' But the sophist takes this same sentence and divides it after 'ἕν,' (by pause or punctuation), in which case it may be rendered 'The Rational one is a proprium of man.'

102,3-4. Gabler's text is hopelessly corrupt, for there are two occurrences of 'ὄρος,' and none of 'ὅρος.' Presumably the fallacy occurs when it is written without accentuation added or pronounced indistinctly, but for the purposes of illustration the accents are shown. Standard examples of the fallacy Accent turn on the ambiguity between 'ορος' as either 'ὅρος' or 'ὄρος.' One might cite the Anonymous *In Aristotelis Sophisticos Elenchos Paraphrasis*, ed. by M. Hayduck, (Berlin: *C.I.A.G.*, 1883), Vol. XXIII, Pts. 1-2, p. 9, ll. 3-4: 'The logical mortal animal is a definition (ὅρος). The hill (ὄρος) stands. Thus, the logical mortal animal stands.' A similar example is at Ps.-Alexander (*Commentarius*), p. 33, ll. 3-5.

It seems reasonable to suppose that Galen is providing an example akin to these. Hence, with some justification we might accept Gabler's possible reconstruction of the text (as included in his 'Observationes,' p. 24), and accordingly read *102,3-4* as follows:

καὶ εἰ ὅρος ἐνταῦθα ἔστηκεν ὅ<που ἐστὶ> τὸ χωρίον·
ὅρος δ' ἐνταῦθα οὐχ ἔστηκεν· <χωρίον ἄρα ἐνταῦθα οὐκ ἔστιν>.

Literally it may be rendered: 'If the boundary stands there where the estate stands but a hill does not stand there, hence the estate is not there.' As such, the consequent is not even an independent assertion. But if we reverse the order of the first premise (to make it otherwise valid), and transform it so as to give it syllogistic form, the sophism may be read as follows:

(1) If his estate is there, then the boundary (ὅρος) stands there.
(2) A hill (ὅρος) does not stand there.
∴ (3) His estate is not there, (by modus tollens).

Clearly, in the second premise the sophist is trading on the ambiguity of 'ορος,' and reasoning as if it had the same meaning as 'ορος' in the first premise, which it does not.

102,9-11. The translation given for this passage disregards Gabler's additions of 'τό' and 'οὐκ ἀκριβῶς,' and at the suggestion of Prof. DeLacy adds 'ὧν' after 'εἰσιν,' and 'οἱ' after 'εἶδος' in line 11, so that it reads as follows after Gabler's dagger:

οἱ μὲν γάρ εἰσιν, <ὧν> τὸ εἶδος <οἱ> σοφισταὶ βιάζονται.

Those which are the same are the cases of actual ambiguity, which the sophists do violence to by taking them in distinct senses, though preserving their form intact. Apparently the first occurrence of 'οἱ' in *102,10* refers anaphorically not only to 'λόγοι,' but also to 'ὀνόματα' in *102,10*. Although 'οἱ' is not exactly an attributive adjective, it may behave like one. On the agreement of attributive adjective with the nearest of two substantives with different genders, see Smyth, p. 275, sec. 1030.

102,16. The question of the reference of 'κἀξ ἄλλων' ('and from other treatises') has not been discussed, much less determined by previous Galenic scholarship. See *supra* p. 46 for my suggestion.

102,18. Textual corruption at *102,18* has tempted Gabler to change the Ambrosian, Aldine, and Basel 'οὖν' to 'οὐκ' and to insert 'ἂν ἄλλως συμβαίη' at *102,18*. This last emendation is inspired by Galen's locution at *102,1*, that fallacies due to language 'otherwise would not arise' than by the sophists' trading on the ambiguity in their component sentences, and this alteration seems acceptable.

104,1. As we recall from the *Institutio Logica* 1. 4, Galen defines a syllogism as 'the entire form of speech through which, when certain things are agreed to, a conclusion is inferred' (translation by John S. Kieffer). Thus, for Galen a syllogism may be an Aristotelian categorical, a Stoic hypothetical, or one of his own relational syllogisms. On this topic, see Galen's *Institutio Logica* 7. 1-3 and 16. 1.

104,3-4. Gabler's insertion here is acceptable, given the sense of the passage. Galen tolerates the hiatus that is created between 'εἴη' and 'ὑπάρχειν.' On this, see Gabler, p. xiv.

106,1. Through *108,13*, this chapter appears in SVF II, #153.

106,7. 'διαφοραί' here refers to the distinctions that the Stoics make in their analysis of ambiguity, and 'διαφορά' is rendered 'kind' to distinguish it from the Galenic 'εἶδος' ('species') or 'τρόπος' ('mode').

106,8. It seems reasonable to suppose that the more subtle gentlemen of the Stoa, the expounders of the teaching Galen adumbrates in Chapter 4, are Chrysippus and his followers, especially Diogenes of Babylonia. Other possible candidates are Zeno of Citium, who is reported to have written two books on *Elenchus* (Diog. Laert. 7. 4, also SVF I, #41), and Sphaerus, a contemporary of Chrysippus and fellow student of Cleanthes. Sphaerus is said to have written one treatise on the subject of ambiguity, entitled 'Περὶ ἀμφιβολιῶν,' (Diog. Laert. 7. 178, also SVF I, #620). That Galen is referring to Zeno is unlikely because of the degree of systematization in the Stoic enumeration—such refinement is a mark of later (Chrysippean) endeavor.

The following considerations militate against the view that Sphaerus is one of the philosophers Galen is referring to here: Galen's terminology in the first part of Chapter 4 (before *108,10*) is strikingly different from what has preceded in the treatise.

For example, he uses 'ἀμφιβολία' as a general term for ambiguity, whereas earlier it refers strictly to the mode of actual syntactic ambiguity. It seems plain that Galen is writing this chapter with a Stoic document in hand, from which he is quoting (or at least paraphrasing). Now there seems good reason to believe that this Stoic source is one of Chrysippus' seven treatises on ambiguity (Diog. Laert. 7. 193., also SVF II, #14) which collectively consist of seventeen books on the subject, or at least a handbook based on this Chrysippean teaching. However, more than one distinguished gentleman is referred to by Galen, ('ὀνομάζουσι' at *106,9* is plural), and it seems reasonable to suppose that this or these person(s) are in agreement with Chrysippus on this doctrine. Hence, it is my view that these more subtle Stoics are Chrysippus and his followers. Sphaerus is unlikely as one of these men, because he was not one of Chrysippus' followers, but a rival Stoic.

Probably one of these followers is Diogenes of Babylonia, to whom von Arnim ascribes the Stoic definition of ambiguity (Diog. Laert. 7. 62, also SVF III, #24, p. 214, ll. 1-5, and see *supra* p. 59). The above is consistent with von Arnim's suggestion that the whole Stoic discussion in *De Captionibus* is probably drawn from Chrysippus' 'Περὶ ἀμφιβολιῶν,' (SVF II, p. 46n.).

106,9. I accept the Kalbfleisch-Gabler alteration, 'εἰρομένου,' from 'εἴρω' ('to string alone'), rather than the Ambrosian MS. and the Aldine, von Arnim, and Kühn editions' 'εἰρημένου,' from 'ἐρῶ' ('to say').

106,10. It is unclear why Gabler employs majuscules or capital letters in *scriptura continua* for some examples (like the present one) and not for others (e.g., at *108,6*). The other editions consistently use only minuscules or lower case Greek letters.

106,14. 'πτῶσις' here means 'case' in the sense of a particular instantiation; e.g., a case of measles. Here a case of man is some particular man. Galen is not referring to grammatical case by 'πτῶσις' here, though he does so at *110,8*. (For more on the subject of the Stoics on grammatical case, see H. Steinthal, (*Geschichte*), pp. 301ff., and A. A. Long, 'Language and Thought in Stoicism,' in *Problems in Stoicism*, ed. by A. A. Long (London: The Athlone Press, 1971), pp. 104-06.)

Steinthal (p. 304) suggests this ontological sense of 'πτῶσις' for the Stoics. He argues that they believe a πτῶσις is the sole reality which we encounter (προσπίπτειν, τυγχάνειν) in contrast to general qualities (γενικὸν ποιόν) or other abstractions which are ἀσώματα (incorporeals). (Οὐσία as essence in the Aristotelian sense, I propose, is just such an abstraction for the Stoics, and is the natural contrast to πτῶσις at *106,14*.) Steinthal cites fragments which suggest this view, one of which is 'Χρύσιππος τὸ μὲν γενικὸν ἡδὺ νοητόν, τὸ δὲ εἰδικὸν προσπίπτον ἡδὺ αἰσθητόν,' ('Chrysippus (says) the generic pleasant is conceivable, but that the specific and encountered pleasant is perceivable,' (my translation; Steinthal cites Prantl, p. 420, n. 58 for this fragment, which may be found in John Stobaeus *Anthologica* Vol. I, ed. by C. Wachsmuth, (Berlin: Weidmann, 1958), p. 477, ll. 1-2).

In *Die Prinzipien der Stoischen Grammatik* (Rostock, 1943), p. 98, Hans-Erich Müller cites two passages in which 'πτῶσις' has the same meaning as *'Fall'* in German, that is, 'a particular case.' They are from the *Scholia in Dionysius Thrax' Ars Grammatica (Grammatici Graeci* I, 3, ed. by A. Hilgard (Leipzig: Teubner, 1901): καθὸ μὲν γὰρ πέπτωκεν ἀπὸ τοῦ κοινοῦ εἰς ἰδιότητα, ὀνομάζεται πτῶσις (p. 231, l. 22), and ὅτι πέπτωκεν ἐκ τοῦ ἀσωμάτου καὶ γενικοῦ εἰς τὸ εἰδικόν, (p. 383, l. 5). In these parallel passages, a πτῶσις is a particular case or instantiation, 'das einzelne besondere "Fallen" des Allgemeinen, das "Vorkommen" des Allgemeinen,' (Müller, p. 93). Hence, there is some external evidence to support the interpretation that a πτῶσις for the Stoics at times designates a specific case of a univeral, like Man.

106,14-16. I accept Gabler's reading, 'σός ἐστιν υἱός' which is inspired by *Soph. El.* 14. 179b39-180a7. Liddell and Scott list no suitable sense of 'τὸ διὰ μέσου;' (see LSJ s.v. μέσος IIId, where 'τὸ διὰ μέσου' is said to mean 'middle,' and 'διὰ μέσου,' 'the use of parenthesis' as a figure of speech). It appears to be a rare Stoic technical term, occurring nowhere else in the doxographical tradition. The sense of the passage suggests its rendering as 'mediating term.'

106,16. It may be noted that in French, unlike Greek, a pleonastic *ne* (i.e., one which does not negate an infinitive or clause in secondary sequence), can be distinguished from the *ne* as an ordinary sign of negation, for *pas* regularly follows the *ne* when negation is intended.

106,17-108,1. 'ἀμφίδοξος' occurs here for the only time in this treatise. Presumably it is a Stoic variant of 'ἀμφίβολος,' meaning 'ambiguous.'

108,1-3. In Galen's report, what I term 'Insignificant Part Construal' is described as the ambiguity which arises from the failure (of a sentence) to make clear which insignificant part is construed with what. I conjecture that the Stoics use the term 'μόριον' here, instead of 'μέρος' because 'μόριον' has a broader sense—a μόριον is any constituent part (of a sentence, for example), whereas 'μέρος' for the Stoics (in a grammatical context) would indicate a part of speech, (see Diog. Laert. 7. 57). Hence a letter, syllable, or perhaps even a connective counts as an insignificant μόριον, but at least on Galen's view, punctuation, pause, and accentuation is excluded.

108,3-4. The tradition is corrupt at *108,3* and von Arnim's restoration of the example which occurs there (accepted by Gabler), which is based on *Iliad* 23. 382, seems correct. Furthermore, Gabler's additions of 'ἤ' at *108,3*, and 'ἤ πρῶτον ἤ τελευταῖον' and 'ἤ' at *108,4* capture precisely the sense of the Stoic explanation of the example's ambiguity. According to the Gabler reconstruction, the Stoics tell us that what is ambiguous in 'ΚΑΙΝΥΚΕΝΗ-ΠΑΡΕΛΑΣΣΕΝ' is that the letter or element η could occur (be construed) as the first or final letter of a word (as 'ἧπαρ' ('liver') or 'κενή' ('void') respectively) or as a disjunctive connective (a διαζευκτικόν). See *supra* p. 66, n. 51, for the Stoic definition of 'διαζευκτικόν.' Clearly, η, a letter, is the insignificant part capable of being construed in more than one way.

108,4-6. 'Significant Part Construal' names a kind of ambiguity which is due to the failure of a sentence to make plain what significant constituent part is construed with what. These μόρια are words (excluding connectives, see *supra* p. 66, n. 51, since connectives do not signify) and perhaps even phrases. Galen omits any explanation for the example he provides of the Stoic type of ambiguity, and this together with the fact that the example at *108,6* is the same one Galen himself uses to illustrate the mode Combination and Division (at *88,18*, which is straight from Aristotle's *Soph. El.* 4. 166ᵃ37-38), leads one to believe that Galen has decided to ignore the Stoics' own example (whatever that may have been). As far as Galen is concerned, 'Πεντήκοντ' ἀνδρῶν ἑκατὸν λίπε δῖος Ἀχιλλεύς' is sufficient as far as exemplifying 'Significant Part Construal.'

108,7-8. The tradition is corrupt here. The Charterian, Kühn, von Arnim, and Gabler 'δηλοῦσα τί' seems preferable to the Ambrosian, Aldine, and Basel 'δηλονότι' at *108,7*. The Charterian, Kühn, von Arnim, and Gabler reading of the example at *108,8* as 'ΔΙΩΝΘΕΩΝΕΣΤΙΝ' is warranted by the explanation that follows at *108,8-9*: The Ambrosian MS. reads 'εὕρω,' and the Aldine and Basel editions have 'εὕρων,' for 'ΕΣΤΙΝ.' In contrast to the example provided for the seventh kind of Stoic ambiguity, this example is typically Stoic by virtue of the use of the names 'Dion' and 'Theon' which occur frequently in Stoic discussions. For example, see Sext. Emp. *Adv. Math.* 8. 12, Diog. Laert. 7. 73-79, and SVF II, #397.

108,9. On one reading of the example in question, it refers to the 'ὕπαρξις,' ('existence') of both men. A. A. Long (in 'Language and Thought in Stoicism,' p. 89), specifies the following senses of 'ὑπάρχειν,' in philosophical Greek: '(1) "exist" in contrast with appear or seem; (2) "be the case" (be true); (3) "be present in" or "be predicated of" a subject; (4) "be real" or "be genuine."' I take 'ὕπαρξις' here, the abstract nominalization of 'ὑπάρχειν,' to signify "existence."

110,12. Gabler's emendation here, the alteration of the tradition's 'θέσιν' to 'σύνθεσιν' seems plausible. I take the expression 'παρὰ τὴν σύνθεσιν' at *110,12* to be elliptical for 'παρὰ τὴν σύνθεσιν καὶ διαίρεσιν,' which occurs at *88,15-16* and at *98,17*. Gabler agrees with this interpretation; (see his 'Index Verborum,' s.v. 'σύνθεσις,' p. 35).

BIBLIOGRAPHY OF ANCIENT AND MODERN SOURCES

A. ANCIENT SOURCES

Alexander of Aphrodisias. *Commentaria in Aristotelis Topicorum Libros Octo*. Edited by M. Wallies. (*Commentaria in Aristotelem Graeca*, Vol. II. Pt. 2) Berlin: Reimer, 1891.
Aristotle. *Analytica Posteriora*. Translated by G. R. G. Mure. London: Oxford University Press, 1928.
———. *Analytica Priora*. Translated by A. J. Jenkinson. London: Oxford University Press, 1928.
———. *Aristotle On Fallacies or the Sophistici Elenchi*. Translated and annotated by Edward Poste. London: Macmillan and Co., 1866.
———. *Ars Rhetorica*. Edited by W. D. Ross. Oxford: Clarendon Press, 1959.
———. *'Art' of Rhetoric*. Translated by J. H. Freese (Loeb Classical Library). Cambridge, Mass.: Harvard University Press, 1926.
———. *Categoriae et Liber De Interpretatione*. Edited by L. Minio-Paluello. Oxford: Clarendon Press, 1949.
———. *De Arte Poetica Liber*. Edited by R. Kassel. Oxford: Clarendon Press, 1965.
———. *Metaphysica*. Translated by W. D. Ross. 2nd. ed. Oxford: Clarendon Press, 1928.
———. *On Sophistical Refutations*. Translated by E. S. Forster (Loeb Classical Library). Cambridge, Mass.: Harvard University Press, 1955.
———. *Organon*. Edited by T. Waitz. 2 vols. Leipzig: Hahn, 1844-46.
———. *Posterior Analytics and Topica*. Translated by H. Tredennick and E. S. Forster (Loeb Classical Library). Cambridge, Mass.: Harvard University Press, 1960.
———. *Prior and Posterior Analytics*. Edited by W. D. Ross. Oxford: Clarendon Press, 1965.
———. *Fragmenta Selecta*. Edited by W. D. Ross. Oxford: Clarendon Press, 1955.
———. *Topica and De Sophisticis Elenchis*. Translated by W. A. Pickard-Cambridge. London: Oxford University Press, 1928.
———. *Topica et Sophistici Elenchi*. Edited by W. D. Ross. Oxford: Clarendon Press, 1970.
Arnim, J. von, ed. *Stoicorum Veterum Fragmenta*. 4 vols. Leipzig: Teubner, 1903-24.
Cicero. *De Natura Deorum, Academica*. Translated by H. Rackham (Loeb Classical Library). Cambridge, Mass.: Harvard University Press, 1933.
Diogenes Laertius. *Lives of Eminent Philosophers*. Translated by R. D. Hicks (Loeb Classical Library). 2 vols. Cambridge, Mass.: Harvard University Press, 1925.
———. *Vitae Philosophorum*. Edited by H. S. Long. 2 vols. Oxford: Clarendon Press, 1964.
Dionysius Thrax. *Ars Grammatica*. Edited by G. Uhlig. (*Grammatici Graeci*, Vol. I, Pt. 1) Leipzig: Teubner, 1883.
Galen. *De Placitis Hippocratis et Platonis*. Edited by Iwan Müller. Leipzig: Teubner, 1874.

―――. *Institutio Logica*. Edited by K. Kalbfleisch. Leipzig: Teubner, 1896.
―――. *Libellus de Captionibus quae per Dictionem Fiunt*. Edited by Carl Gabler. Rostock, 1903.
―――. *On the Natural Faculties*. Translated by A. J. Brock (Loeb Classical Library). Cambridge, Mass.: Harvard University Press, 1916.
―――. *On the Passions and Errors of the Soul*. Translated by Paul W. Harkins, with an Introduction and Interpretation by Walther Riese. Columbus: Ohio State University Press, 1963.
―――. *Opera Omnia*. Edited by C. G. Kühn. 20 vols. Leipzig, 1821-33.
―――. *Scripta Minora*. Edited by J. Marquardt, I. Müller, and G. Helmreich. 3 vols. Leipzig: Teubner, 1884.
Gellius, Aulus. *The Attic Nights of Aulus Gellius*. Translated by J. C. Rolfe (Loeb Classical Library). 3 vols. Cambridge, Mass.: Harvard University Press, 1946.
In Aristotelis Sophisticos Elenchos Paraphrasis (Anonymus). Edited by M. Hayduck (*Commentaria in Aristotelem Graeca*, Vol. XXIII, Pts. 1-2) Berlin: Reimer, 1883.
Plato. *Opera*. Edited by John Burnet. 5 vols. Oxford: Clarendon Press, 1900-07.
―――. *Phaedrus*. Translated, with an Introduction by W. C. Helmbold and W. G. Rabinowitz. New York: Library of Liberal Arts Press, 1956.
―――. *The Republic of Plato*. Translated with an Introduction and Notes by F. M. Cornford. New York and London: Oxford University Press, 1945.
Ps.-Alexander. *In Aristotelis Sophisticos Elenchos Commentarium*. Edited by M. Wallies. (*Commentaria in Aristotelem Graeca*, Vol. II, Pt. 3) Berlin: Reimer, 1898.
Sextus Empiricus. *Opera*. Edited by H. Mutschmann. Leipzig: Teubner, 1912-14.
―――. *Sextus Empiricus*. Translated by R. G. Bury (Loeb Classical Library). 4 vols. 1933-49.
Simplicius. *In Aristotelis Physicorum Libros Quattuor Posteriores Commentaria*. Edited by H. Diels (*Commentaria in Aristotelem Graeca*, Vol. X, Pts. 5-8) Berlin: Reimer, 1895.
Stobaeus, John. *Anthologica*. Edited by C. Wachsmuth. 2 vols. Berlin: Weidmann, 1958.

B. MODERN SOURCES

Alston, William P. *Philosophy of Language*. Englewood Cliffs: Prentice-Hall, Inc., 1964.
Austin, J. L. *How To Do Things with Words*. Edited by J. O. Urmson. Galaxy Books. New York: Oxford University Press, 1965.
Bellert, Irena, and Hiż, Henry. 'Paraphrastic Sets and Grammatical Analysis, Part. I.' *University of Pennsylvania Transformations and Discourse Analysis Papers*, No. 59, 1965.
Black, Max. *The Labyrinth of Language*. Mentor Books. New York and Toronto: New American Library, 1968.
Bocheński, I. M. *La Logique de Théophraste*. Fribourg: Collectanea Friburgensia, 1947.
Bowersock, G. W. *Greek Sophists in the Roman Empire*. Oxford: Clarendon Press, 1969.

Buck, Carl D. *Comparative Grammar of Greek and Latin*. Chicago: University of Chicago Press, 1933.
Carroll, Lewis. *The Annotated Alice: Alice's Adventures in Wonderland and Through the Looking Glass*. Edited by Martin Gardner. Forum Books. New York: World Publishing Co., 1963.
Copi, I. M. *Introduction to Logic*. 4th ed. New York: The Macmillan Co., 1972.
Coxe, J. R. *The Writings of Hippocrates and Galen*. Philadelphia: Lindsay and Blakiston, 1846.
Cranz, F. Edward. 'Alexander Aphrodisiensis.' *Catalogus Translationum et Commentariorum: Mediaeval and Renaissance Latin Translations and Commentaries*. Edited by Paul Oskar Kristeller. Washington, D. C.: Catholic University of America Press, 1960.
DeLacy, Phillip. 'Galen and the Greek Poets.' *Greek, Roman, and Byzantine Studies*, VII (1966), 259-66.
———. 'Plato and the Method of the Arts.' *The Classical Tradition: Literary and Historical Studies in Honor of Harry Caplan*. Edited by Luitpold Wallach. Ithaca: Cornell University Press, 1966.
Edlow, R. Blair.' The Stoics on Ambiguity.' *Journal of the History of Philosophy*, XIII (October, 1975), 423-35.
Empson, William. *Seven Types of Ambiguity*. 3rd ed. New York: New Directions Publishing Corp., 1966.
Fillmore, Charles J. 'A Case for Case.' *Universals in Linguistic Theory*. Edited by E. Bach and R. T. Harms. New York: Holt, Rinehart and Winston, 1968.
Flew, Anthony. 'Introduction,' *Logic and Language*. Edited by Anthony Flew. 1st and 2nd series, Anchor Books. Garden City: Doubleday & Co., 1965.
Forbes, P. B. R. 'Greek Pioneers in Philology and Grammar.' *Classical Review*, XLVII (July, 1933), 105-12.
Gilbert, Neal W. *Renaissance Concepts of Method*. New York: Columbia University Press, 1960.
Grube, G. M. A. *The Greek and Roman Critics*. Toronto: University of Toronto Press, 1965.
C. L. Hamblin. *Fallacies*. University Paperbacks. London and New York: Methuen & Co., 1970.
Hintikka, Jaakko. 'Aristotle and the Ambiguity of Ambiguity.' *Inquiry*, II (Autumn, 1959), 137-51.
———. 'Different Kinds of Equivocation in Aristotle.' *Journal of the History of Philosophy*, IX (July, 1971), 368-72.
———. 'Time, Truth, and Knowledge in Ancient Greek Philosophy.' *American Philosophical Quarterly*, IV (January, 1967), 1-11.
Hockett, Charles F. *A Course in Modern Linguistics*. New York: The Macmillan Company, 1958.
Jannaris, A. N. *An Historical Greek Grammar*. London: Macmillan and Co., 1897.
———. 'Plato's Testimony to Quantity and Accent.' *American Journal of Philology*, XXIII (1902), 75-83.
Joseph, H. W. B. *An Introduction to Logic*. Oxford: Clarendon Press, 1906.
Kapp, Ernst. *Greek Foundations of Traditional Logic*. New York: Columbia University Press, 1942.
Kieffer, John S. *Galen's Institutio Logica: English Translation, Introduction,*

and Commentary. Baltimore: The Johns Hopkins University Press, 1964.
Kneale, William, and Kneale, Martha. *The Development of Logic.* Oxford: Clarendon Press, 1962.
Long, A. A. 'Language and Thought in Stoicism.' *Problems in Stoicism.* Edited by A. A. Long. London: The Athlone Press, 1971.
Łukasiewicz, Jan. 'Philosophische Bemerkungen zu mehrwertigen Systemen des Aussagenkalkuls.' *Comptes Rendus des Séances de la Société des Sciences et des Lettres de Varsovie,* Vol. XXIII. 1930, 51-77.
Lyons, John. *Introduction to Theoretical Linguistics.* Cambridge: Cambridge University Press, 1968.
Mates, Benson. *Stoic Logic.* Berkeley and Los Angeles: University of California Press, 1953.
Mau, Jürgen. *Galen, Einführung in die Logik: Kritisch-exegetischer Kommentar mit deutscher Übersetzung.* Berlin: Deutsche Akademie der Wissenschaften, 1960.
Mill, J. S. *Utilitarianism.* Edited by O. Piest. 2nd. rev. ed. New York: Library of Liberal Arts Press, 1957.
Müller, Hans-Erich. *Die Prinzipien der Stoischen Grammatik.* Rostock. 1943.
Müller, Iwan. 'Über Galens Werk vom wissenschaftlichen Beweis.' *Abhandlungen der Philosophisch-Philologischen Klasse der Königlich Bayerischen Akademie der Wissenschaften.* Vol. XX. Munich, 1897, 405-78.
Nuchelmans, Gabriel. *Theory of the Proposition.* Amsterdam: North Holland Publishing Co., 1973.
Owen, G. E. L. 'Logic and Metaphysics in Some Earlier Works of Aristotle. '*Aristotle and Plato in the Mid-Fourth Century.* Edited by I. Düring and G. E. L. Owen. Göteborg: Studia Graeca et Latina, 1960.
——. 'Aristotle on the Snares of Ontology.' *New Essays on Plato and Aristotle.* Edited by Renford Bambrough. London: Routledge & Kegan Paul, 1965.
Prantl, Carl. *Geschichte der Logik im Abendland.* 4 vols. Leipzig: Hirzl, 1855-70.
Quine, W. V. O. *Elementary Logic.* rev. ed. Cambridge, Mass.: Harvard University Press, 1966.
——. *Word and Object.* Cambridge, Mass.: M.I.T. Press, 1960.
Robinson, R., and Denniston, J. D. 'Plato.' *Plato: Metaphysics and Epistemology.* Edited by Gregory Vlastos. Anchor Books. Garden City: Doubleday and Co., 1971.
Ross, David. *Aristotle.* University Paperbacks. London and New York: Methuen & Co., 1964.
Russell, Bertrand. *Human Knowledge: Its Scope and Limits.* Clarion Books. New York: Simon and Schuster, 1948.
Ryle, Gilbert. 'Dialectic in the Academy.' *New Essays on Plato and Aristotle.* Edited by Renford Bambrough. London: Routledge & Kegan Paul, 1965.
Sandys, John E. *A History of Classical Scholarship.* 3 vols. 3rd ed. Cambridge: Cambridge University Press, 1921.
Sarton, George. *Galen of Pergamon.* Lawrence: University of Kansas Press, 1954.
Schmidt, Rudolph. *Stoicorum Grammatica.* Halle: Eduard Anton, 1839.
Smyth, H. W. *Greek Grammar.* Cambridge, Mass.: Harvard University Press, 1956.

Steinthal, H. *Geschichte der Sprachwissenschaft bei den Griechen und Römern*. 2nd ed. Berlin: Ferd Dummlers, 1890.
Wehrli, Fritz. *Eudemos von Rhodos: Die Schule des Aristoteles, Texte und Kommentar*. Basel: Benno Schwabe & Co., 1955.
Zeller, Eduard. *Outlines of the History of Greek Philosophy*. Revised by W. Nestle and translated by L. Palmer. Meridian Books. 13th ed. Cleveland: World Publishing Co., 1969.
——. *The Stoics, Epicureans and Sceptics*. Translated by O. J. Reichel. New York: Russell & Russell, 1962.

INDEX

Accent, fallacy of, 26-28; as Galenic mode of ambiguity, 40, 44-45
Alexander of Aphrodisias, 118
Ambiguity, actual, 42-43; apparent, 45-47; contemporary definition of, 13-15; lexical, 41; potential, 42-45; Stoic definition of, 59; syntactic, 41-42
Amphiboly, fallacy of, 22-23; as Galenic mode of ambiguity, 42
Apollonius Dyscolus, 126
Aristotle, on ambiguity, 17-31; on defining *'logos'*, 127
Arnim, J. von, 56, 135

Bellert, I., 12
Black, M., 9
Bocheński, I. M., 4

Chellas, B., 15
Chrysippus, 4, 56-58, 61, 81, 132-34
Cicero, 57
Cleanthes, 132
Combination, fallacy of, 24; and Division, as Galenic mode of ambiguity, 40, 42-43
Copi, I. M., 45
Cox, J. R., 4

DeLacy, P., ix, 125, 128, 131
Diocles of Magnesia, 59, 125
Diogenes Laertius, 56-59, 66-67, 117, 127, 132-36
Diogenes of Babylonia, 61, 81, 132-33
Dionysius Thrax, 127, 134
Division, fallacy of, 24-25

Electra sophism, 57
Empson, W., 14
Eudemus of Rhodes, 54-55

Fallacies, *extra dictionem*, 19-21; *in dictione*, 19, 21-28
Focal meaning, 17, 29-31
Form of expression, fallacy of, 23-24; as Galenic modes of ambiguity, 40, 45-47

Gabler, C., xiii, 4, 87, 125, 129-30, 133, 136
Galen, career of, 4-8, on language, 32-39; on ambiguity, 40-48
Gellius, Aulus, 18, 54, 57
Gilbert, N., 7, 53, 128

Hamblin, C. L., 4
Heraclitus, 47
Hintikka, J., 11, 16
Hippocrates, 5
Hiż, H., 12
Hockett, C. F., 32
Homonymy, fallacy of, 21-22; as Galenic mode of ambiguity, 40-41, 79; in the Stoic theory, 61-67, 81-83
Horned Man sophism, 57

Ignoratio Elenchi, 19-21
Institutio Logica, 3, 46, 125, 132

Jannaris, A. N., 28, 43, 118
Joseph, H. W. B., 21, 27, 51-52, 117

Kahn, C., ix, 80
Kalbfleisch, K., 4, 118, 123, 126
Kapp, E., 6
Kieffer, J., 3, 132
Kneale, W., and Kneale, M., xi, 3, 6, 56-57

Lexical identity, Aristotle on, 28; Galen on, 44
Lexis, 32
Liar sophism, 56-57
Linguistic confusion, 19, 21, 24-28
Long, A. A., 133, 136
Lukasiewicz, J., xi
Lyons, J., 13-14

Mates, B., xi, 56
Mau, J., 3
Megarian School, 56
Method of division, 49-53
Michael of Ephesus, 118
Mill, J. S., 24
Multiple applicability, 10

Nature-convention controversy, 123-24
Nobody sophism, 58, 65-66

Owen, G. E. L., 11, 29

Paraphrase values, 12-13
Parrot, Cecil, 32, 65
Plato, 4-5, 33, 47, 49-50, 52-53, 74, 122-24, 126-27
Prantl, C., 4-5, 54-55
Ps.-Alexander, 25, 117-22, 127, 129, 131

Quine, W. V. O., 10, 13, 42, 46-48, 57, 64-65, 128-29

Russell, B., 33
Ryle, G., 18

Sarton, G., 3
Sandys, J. E., 3, 28
Schmidt, R., xi
Scriptura continua, 28, 129
Sentence, as defined by Plato, 37, 127; as defined by Aristotle, Dionysius Thrax, and Ps.-Alexander, 127
Sentential identity, Aristotle on, 26; Galen on, 44
Sextus Empiricus, 58, 60, 120, 136
Sophistical refutation, definition of, 18
Sophists, 122-23
Sorites sophism, 57
Sophistici Elenchi, 17-28, 62, 69-71, 135
Speech acts, 11, 39
Sphaerus, 132-33
Stoics, leading theorists, 132-33, on ambiguity, 56-68, 135
Steinthal, H., xi, 133-34

Vagueness, 10

Wagon sophism, 57
Wehrli, F., 54

Zeller, E., xi, 5
Zeno of Citium, 122, 132